You _____ and _____

Can build a beautiful and loving marriage.

Here's how.

Courtship *After* Marriage

Courtship *After* Marriage

Zig Ziglar

A Division of Thomas Nelson Publishers
Nashville

Published in Nashville, Tennessee, by Oliver-Nelson Books, a division of Thomas Nelson, Inc.

Scripture quotations noted KJV are from The King James Version of the Holy Bible. Scripture quotations noted NIV are taken from the HOLY BIBLE: NEW INTERNATIONAL VERSION. Copyright © 1973, 1978, 1984 by the International Bible Society. Used by permission of Zondervan Bible Publishers. Scripture quotations noted EB are taken from The Everyday Bible, New Century Version, copyright © 1987 by Worthy Publishing, Fort Worth, Texas 76137. Used by permission.

CHAPTER 2. Excerpt from "Ten-Cow Wife" in Man of Steel and Velvet by Aubrey P. Andelin. Copyright 1972, Pacific Press, Santa Barbara, Calif. Used by permission. CHAPTER 4. Excerpt from Dr. Dobson: Turning Hearts Toward Home by Rolf Zettersten, Copyright 1989, Word, Inc., Dallas, Texas. Used by permission. CHAPTER 6. Excerpt from Secrets of Closing the Sale by Zig Ziglar. Copyright 1984, Fleming H. Revell, Old Tappan, N.J. Reprinted by permission. CHAPTER 8. Excerpt from Family Altar, Devotions for Every Day of the Year by F. W. Herzberger. Used by permission. Paraphrases from Man of Steel and Velvet by Aubrey P. Andelin. Copyright 1972, Pacific Press, Santa Barbara, Calif. Used by permission. CHAPTER 9. Excerpt from Executive Excellence by Steven Covey. Copyright 1988; also Principle-Centered Leadership, copyright 1990, The Institute for Principle-Centered Leadership. Excerpt from His Needs, Her Needs by Willard F. Harley, Jr., Fleming H. Revell, Old Tappan, N.J. Reprinted by permission. Excerpt from Richard Exley, Perils of Power—Immorality in the Ministry (Tulsa: Honor Books, 1988), pp. 26–27. Used by permission. CHAPTER 10. Quotation by Mary Kay Ash from the copyrighted article "Workaholics Beware: Long Hours May Not Pay" in U.S. News & World Report, 7 April 1986. CHAPTER 11. Excerpt from Two Become One by J. Allan Petersen. Published by Tyndale House Publishers, copyright Family Concern, Inc. Used by permission. All rights reserved. Excerpt from Homemade, vol. 10, no. 12, Morrison, Colo. Used by permission.

Every effort has been made to contact the owners or owners' agents of copyrighted material for permission to use their material. If copyrighted material has been included without the correct copyright notice or without permission, due to error or failure to locate owners/agents or otherwise, we apologize for the error or omission and ask that the owner or owner's agent contact Oliver-Nelson and supply appropriate information. Correct information will be included in any reprinting.

Printed in the United States of America.

Library of Congress Cataloging-in-Publication Data

Ziglar, Zig.
    Courtship after marriage : romance can last a lifetime / Zig Ziglar.
        p.   cm.
    Includes bibliographical references.
    ISBN 0-8407-9111-9
    ISBN 0-7852-6724-7 (Repkg.)
     1. Marriage—United States.   2. Courtship—United States.
3. Marriage—Religious aspects—Christianity. I. Title.
HQ734.Z54   1990
646.7 ′8—dc20   90–39257
                                     CIP

4 5 6 7 8 9 10 — 04 03 02 01 00

To
Jean Abernathy Ziglar
(The Redhead)

Courtship After Marriage is a *tribute* to the most loving, loyal, insightful, and supportive person I have ever known. She has taught me much about love, marriage, and courtship while demonstrating that romance *can* last a lifetime and grow deeper and more beautiful with each passing day.

I love you, Sweetheart.

Zig Ziglar

CONTENTS

THANK YOU

When you start to say "thank you," your mind turns to the many people who played an important role in an effort such as this one. In this particular case, I would like to start with "The Redhead" who has had a significant role in everything I have done, including this book. I would also like to thank the other members of my family for the patience and understanding they have demonstrated as I have had to skip a few of our cherished family gatherings to put the final touches on this book.

A double portion goes to Don Hawkins who did a considerable amount of the research, contributed a valuable marriage "temperature" questionnaire, and interpreted the results of the questionnaire from the couples who had been married twenty-five years or more and who would marry the same mate again. A special thank you also to Carlos Rosales who designed the grid that enabled Don to interpret and compile the data for the questionnaire.

My heartfelt gratitude goes to Jim Savage, our Senior Vice President, who guided the project from the beginning and whose literary insights and contributions were instrumental in maintaining order and form throughout the book. Along these lines, I'm particularly appreciative of Sue Schuenemann who did such a yeoman job, starting early and staying late, in the typing and retyping of the manuscript. Her obvious delight in working on the book and her encouragement were certainly rewarding to me.

A special thank you to Dr. J. Allan Petersen for the contributions he has made through his books and his publication *Happiness Is Homemade*. Also to Dr. James Dobson, Dr. Richard Furman, Charlie Shedd, and a number of other authors who helped with their research and personal examples. A special thank you also to psychiatrist Paul Meier, who worked with me in designing the questionnaire for the couples who had been happily married twenty-five or more years, and to psychiatrist Frank Minirth and psychologist Charles Lowery who permitted us to use some of their creative efforts. My gratitude also extends to Ron Land, President of Zig Ziglar Corporation, who supplied me with some notable examples and who kept all the fires burning around the corporate offices while these activities were taking place.

INTRODUCTION

Several years ago while coming in on a plane (which is generally the way I fly), I noticed that the fellow seated next to me had his wedding band on the index finger of his right hand. I couldn't resist the temptation so I commented, "Friend, you've got your wedding band on the wrong finger." He responded, "Yeah, I married the wrong woman."

It is far more important to be the right kind of person than it is to marry the right kind of person.

I have no way of knowing whether or not he married the wrong woman, but I do know that many people have a lot of wrong ideas about marriage and what it takes to make that marriage happy and successful. I'll be the first to admit that it's possible that you did marry the wrong person. However, if you treat the wrong person like the right person, you could well end up having married the right person after all. On the other hand, if you marry the right person and treat that person wrong, you certainly will have ended up marrying the wrong person. I also know that it is far more important to *be* the right *kind* of person than it is to marry the right person. In short, whether you married the right or wrong person is primarily up to *you.*

PASSION AND ECSTASY

Research, personal observation, and experience prove that stable, sound marriages are *not* built on the passion of the moment. A state of ecstasy and exhilaration built on emotion and feeling is not an everyday occurrence. Unrealistic expectations create serious problems in many marriages. Realistic (and positive) expectations lead to marriages that last.

Horse sense is just stable thinking.

In pursuing the long-range aspects of marriage, I discovered that a little common "horse sense" (which as you know is just "stable thinking") is required for success in marriage. For example, TRUE HAPPINESS AND REAL LOVE REQUIRE:

- A *daily* effort from husband and wife, including a willingness to forgive and go the extra mile to please your mate (that extra mile will burn 391 calories);
- The acceptance of the fact that in all facets of the successful marriage, the point is not *who* is right but *what* is right;
- The willingness to "eat crow" (no calories here) when you are wrong and to be wise enough and humble enough to ask your mate to forgive you; and when you are the offended party, you must not "force-feed" your mate this "crow";
- The willingness to move from "your" side of the table

to your mate's side, lovingly embracing him or her and healing the wound *together* through the love you are building and the forgiveness you can extend.

SOME EXCITING FACTS TO BE LEARNED_____

As your marriage endures *and* grows, you recognize that the real long-range benefit of a solid marriage comes from the security of knowing you have someone who accepts you, loves you, understands you, is a real helpmate, encourager, and supporter; one who is loyal to you and delights in pleasing you because you have first of all done and been all of those things to your spouse.

With each day you invest in developing a successful marriage, you come to realize that as the ecstasy, exhilaration, and passion of the honeymoon naturally and in an orderly fashion begin to subside, you come to experience a far deeper feeling of exhilaration and real love.

As the years go by, your greatest joy comes when you are able to comfort a hurting mate, to take over additional responsibilities when your mate is physically exhausted or not feeling well enough to carry his or her share of the burden at that particular moment. Your delight increasingly comes from the things you can do for your mate and not what your mate can do for you. You come to realize that dependability, tenderness, affection, nourishing, cherishing, seeking, pleasing, satisfying, and all the "little things" that make marriage such a "big success" clearly identify *love*, while the "pleasure only" seekers in life mistakenly believe that fun and games constitute a "real" marriage.

Over the years, the development of these positive qualities within the marriage will make you a better person, a better parent, a more productive worker, a better role model, and the anchor of your family.

BUT WILL "COURTSHIP" WORK FOR ME?_____

Several years ago I got a telephone call from a man in Atlanta who was deeply distressed. His wife of twenty-one years had just asked him for a divorce. He shared with me how much he loved her and said that she really was his life. He told me about their new grandbaby, and mentioned that he felt more like a family than ever before in their married life. He wanted to know if I had any suggestions about how he could save his marriage. Since I had been doing a "Courtship After Marriage" seminar for several years, I promised to send him an audiocassette recording covering much of the material contained in this book. I shared my belief that if both he and his wife would follow through on the suggestions, they could rebuild the relationship that had been a loving one for many years.

Two weeks later I received another call from the gentleman, and this time his wife was on the extension. I don't recall ever hearing two people more enthused, excited, or so obviously in love than those two. We chatted for ten or fifteen minutes, and as we started to say our good-byes, the wife was most gracious in her compliments. She said that what I had shared in the recorded seminar had really worked for them. Then she quietly said, "But, Zig, let me tell you why it worked. You would have no way of knowing, but about a year ago we were at the Fairmont Hotel in Dallas to attend a convention. On Sunday night, after church, you and your Redhead came over to the hotel and were enjoying a bowl of their famous French onion soup.

"There were a number of other people, including us, in the restaurant, but as far as you two were concerned, there was no one else there. You were seated at a table for four; but instead of sitting across from each other, you sat side by side, and your eyes were only for each other. You were holding hands; you put your arm around her; you laughed and, in short, conducted yourselves like two lovebirds who were oblivious to the rest of the world.

"Zig, then I knew you two were practicing what you had been teaching and were obviously in love and having a wonderful time courting each other. To be candid, I was envious of you, yet very hopeful for us. I knew you were onto something that if we followed, we, too, could have not only romance but permanent love in our lives. So, I just want you to know your credibility as you talked about courting your mate was very high with us." She went on to say that she was so glad they had been in the restaurant that Sunday night: "Had we not seen the two of you together, acting as you did, we might not have listened with the same objectivity as we did to your tape."

I share this incident because I want you to know from the beginning that what I'll be sharing has worked wonderfully well for us, and I believe many of the concepts will work for you. Needless to say, we are all unique as individuals, and that uniqueness is magnified through the joining together in holy matrimony of husband and wife, so there will be some obvious variations in results. However, the principles are sound, and with a little creative application, these principles and procedures can have a dramatic impact on your marriage.

BEWARE! _____

One word of caution. Since my nature is upbeat and since I'm inclined to look for the good in every situation, I might be inclined to give you the impression that ours is the perfect marriage. Obviously, that is not the case, and I will point out some of our difficulties as we go along. But I truly believe that we can learn and profit more from positive examples than negative ones, so that's where the emphasis will be.

THE RIGHT INFORMATION _____

In an effort to be sure the concepts, principles, and action steps in this book are practical and applicable—as well as time tested—our staff conducted an extensive (though unscientific) survey of couples who had been married twenty-five years or longer. The results of the survey and the research I studied that was done by others were overwhelmingly clear. The message: The right way is the best way; faithfulness to your mate is prerequisite to success and happiness in the marriage; being gentle and kind in your communications as well as thoughtful and considerate in your actions is truly the romantic *and* practical way to keep the marriage intact *and* keep fun and excitement alive; you "court" each other long after the wedding bells are but a distant and pleasant memory.

This survey is reprinted in the Appendix of this book. Let me challenge you to stop right now and fill in your answers. Regardless of the number of years you have been married, you will get some tremendous insight from evaluating your answers. The survey will also work as a valuable pretest to help you focus on areas you may want to strengthen as you read *Courtship After Marriage*. After you have finished reading this book, retake the last twenty-two questions (45–66) in the survey. If your answers are the same, one of us will have failed.

YOU CAN HAVE IT ALL _____

As you dig deeply into the concepts of this book, you will get more and more excited about the basic philosophy: "You can have everything in life you want if you will just help enough other people get what they want." For example, in *any* marriage that survives, it is *impossible* for only one of the partners to be genuinely happy. Both will be happy, or *neither* will be happy. Without mutual respect, no marriage is going to endure *and* be happy.

In case you think I've suddenly turned dreamer, let me remind you that the hundreds of couples who participated in our survey and the thousands of couples who, in one form or another, provided data and information for much of this book have accomplished the objectives we've just described. Question: If thousands of couples have learned that romance *can* last a lifetime, doesn't it make sense that *you* and your mate can learn the same thing?

As you possibly have heard, I am an incurable optimist (I would go after Moby Dick in a rowboat and take the tartar sauce with me), so I am absolutely convinced that the principles and procedures contained in this book will make a difference not only in your marriage but in America as well. I'm also convinced that love *and* romance can exist and grow in marriage. It does in ours; it can in yours. I wrote this book to show you how *and* assure you that with *Courtship After Marriage, Romance Can Last a Lifetime.*

1 BE HAPPY— YOU'RE MARRIED

> At the end, only two things really matter to a man, regardless of who he is, and they are the affection and understanding of his family. Anything and everything else he creates are insubstantial. They are ships given over to the mercy of the winds and the tides of prejudice, but the family is an everlasting anchorage, a quiet harbor where a man's ships can be left to swing to the moorings of pride and loyalty.
>
> —Admiral Richard Byrd, written on his deathbed

One of the most meaningful experiences of my married life took place after my wife and I had been married for over thirty years. Early one morning as we sat in our bedroom drinking coffee and just greeting the day, neither of us was saying very much. Then she quietly looked at me and said, "You know, Honey, I wish I were younger." And I said, "Well, for goodness sakes, why?" She responded, "If I were younger, I could be married to you even longer."

I'll have to confess, those words moved me as no words have moved me before or since. Never have I felt more loved or more like we were one than at that particular moment. Now, we certainly have had more than our share of special moments. We've been to many beautiful places and shared many exciting experiences, but in the final analysis, the one that has meant the most to me was the one that occurred in our own home on that glorious morning. Love and happiness are not generally found in those faraway places with strange-sounding names. Love is most often found in the home—in the presence of a caring and considerate mate who nurtures love daily.

Courtship After Marriage is written to help men and women from all age groups and in all walks of life find these tender moments and increase their frequency, regardless of the current state of the marriage. You can take a great marriage and make it even better—or a poor marriage and make it great. This is my objective *and* my promise to you!

SOME UNSOLICITED ADVICE

Two "old boys" down home went deer hunting and hit the jackpot. They killed an eleven-point buck and were dragging him through the thick underbrush toward their truck when they encountered another hunter who offered some free and unsolicited advice, "Fellows, it's none of my business, but if you will pull that deer by the horns instead of by the legs, those horns won't get caught in the underbrush, and he will be lots easier to pull."

Recognizing the wisdom involved, combined with their desire to be friendly, they dropped the deer's legs, grabbed him by the horns, and started pulling. After a couple of minutes, one of them commented that their benefactor was one smart guy because the deer *was* much easier to pull. The other "old boy" wasn't so sure about the wisdom, though, as he said, "Yes, but we're getting farther from the truck all the time!"

Of course, it's a joke. However, it's not a joke that many husbands and wives are getting farther apart as the years go by when they should be getting closer together. The net result is that our society and our way of life are all being negatively impacted, and our nation itself, based on historical evidence, is threatened.

IS MARRIAGE IMPORTANT?

British anthropologist John D. Unwin conducted an in-depth study of eighty civilizations that have come and gone over a period of some four thousand years. Dr. Unwin discovered that a common thread ran through all of them. In each instance, they started out with a conservative mind-set involving strong moral values with a heavy emphasis on family. Over a period of time, the conservative mind-set became more and more liberal, moral values declined, and the family suffered. In each instance, as the family deteriorated, the civilization itself started to come apart; and in all eighty cases, the fall of the nation was related to the fall of the family. In most cases, that civilization fell within one generation of the fall of the family unit.

Unwin's research revealed that when a man falls in love with a woman, dedicating himself to care for her and protect her and support her, he suddenly becomes the mainstay of social order. Instead of using his energies to pursue his own lusts and desires, he sweats to build a home and save for the future and seek the best job available. His selfish impulses are inhibited; his sexual passions are channeled. He discovers a sense of pride—yes, masculine pride—because he is needed by his wife and children. Everyone benefits from the relationship.

When a society is composed of millions of individual families established on a morally sound plan of conduct, then the nation is strong and stable. Strength and solidarity are the great contributions marriage makes to civilization. But in the absence of family commitment, ruination is inevitable. When husbands and wives have no reason to harness their energies in support of the home, then drug abuse, alcoholism, sexual promiscuity, job instability, and overly aggressive behavior can be expected to run unchecked throughout the culture. And the lack of focused energies is the beginning of the end.

SOME GOOD NEWS

Countless studies by outstanding (and diverse) scientists, psychologists, and sociologists such as Pitirim Sorokin, Arnold Toynbee, Will and Ariel Durant, William Stevens, Sigmund Freud, James Dobson, and the previously mentioned John Unwin have *proven* there is a positive side to the story.

Civilizations prosper under moral and sexual restraint. Sexual energy is the most creative of all energies, and because of our nature, when we are loyal to our mate, we will have a surplus of this energy. Surplus energy provides an abundance for becoming more productive and more creative and, in general, producing better works of literature and science as well as material goods. Not only does the family benefit from the creative use of this sexual energy, but the energy created is used to raise the standard of living and to advance the quality of life for everyone. The specific use of this surplus sexual energy is done as an unselfish act of love and generosity.

The man or woman, on the other hand, who dissipates sexual energies by extramarital affairs is acting in an irresponsible and selfish manner, seeking only enjoyment without consideration of the damage done to the family and children as well as to the sexual partners and their families. The net result is that creativity is stifled because selfishness does not generate the same kind of creativity that unselfishness does.

MEN ARE SHOW-OFFS

Additionally, man is a natural-born show-off and is highly motivated by recognition and praise from those he truly loves. For years Marabel Morgan led a study and support group made up of the wives of the Miami Dolphins professional football team. She attended all the home games and sat with the wives in a special section of the stadium. During a key game leading into the play-offs, the great Miami quarterback, Bob Griese, passed to Paul Warfield, who ran thirty more yards for the game-winning touchdown. He circled the end zone, spiking the ball in NFL fashion. As he ran along the sidelines, 60,000-plus screaming fans were on their feet, but his eyes were searching the stands for the face of his beloved wife. When their eyes met, he waved to her, and she saluted him with "That's my man!" With the approval of 60,000 fans and millions more watching on television, only one person's approval really mattered. That couple confirmed the truth of this statement: "The affirming, approving, encouraging mate has the power to make even the most ordinary spouse a champion."

In my own case, I firmly believe (based on my own feelings and supported by comments from those who know me best) I am on my tiptoes more and reach my peak performance when I am making a speech and my wife is in the audience. This has nothing to do with effort. I honestly give each presentation my best shot, regardless of the circumstances, but the reality is that my best is better when *she* is there. When I speak, if she is in the audience, if everyone else were to say complimentary things, I would be grateful and appreciative; but the reality is, until she comes to me and says something nice, there is something missing. Praise and recognition from the one you love will definitely enhance the performance of any individual, male or female.

The sad fact is, many men seem to forget that women benefit from praise and recognition as much as men do— *especially* when the accolades come from their mate. Like men, women feel fulfilled and completely loved when they are affirmed by their spouse. Strangely enough, this fact is often overlooked by many husbands, including this one.

Classic example: In the summer of 1989, we added two

enormously successful retired business executives to our Board of Directors at the Zig Ziglar Corporation. Fred Smith and Seth Macon have been instrumental in helping us spread our message more effectively through restructuring the company. In analyzing the abilities of the other members of the Board, they noticed one whose talents and skills were not being used to their full capacity. Fred Smith suggested that we form an audit committee and appoint Jean Ziglar as chairperson of this most important new committee. While I will take some credit in having asked her to serve on the Board, these men immediately recognized her mental alertness and intuitive business insights. She has done a magnificent job, giving me frequent and abundant reason to praise her most sincerely. Question: Where was I while she was serving with commitment and loyalty in the previous years? Sometimes "us husbands" can be dense!

HOW IMPORTANT IS YOUR MATE TO YOUR SUCCESS?

It was fairly late at night when I arrived at my hotel in Richmond, Virginia, in April of 1988. I checked in, picked up my bag, and headed for the elevator. A lady traveler with several bags was about two steps behind me. I pushed the button for the elevator, and as it came up from the basement, I exchanged greetings with her. At that point, the elevator door opened and a smiling, obviously enthusiastic young bellman stepped out and lifted her bags into the elevator, chatting pleasantly as he did so. I waited until he had moved the bags in, then grabbed my bag and stepped into the elevator. As I did, the young bellman looked at me and, with a tremendous burst of enthusiasm, almost shouted my name: "Zig Ziglar!" For the next few seconds he was off on a high that was a sight to behold. He spoke energetically about how glad he was to see me, how I had changed his life, and how I had done so many things for him.

At that point, the bewildered (or was she bemused) lady looked at me and asked, "What on earth do you do?" Before I could answer, the bellman popped out, "He writes books and he makes speeches! As a matter of fact, he is THE GREATEST in the WHOLE WORLD!" That was when the lady coolly asked, "And to what do you attribute your remarkable success?" There was a delay of about one-tenth of a second before the bellman eagerly answered, "The Redhead!" (When I talk about my wife, I call her "The Redhead." When I'm talking to her, it's "Sugar Baby." Her name is Jean.)

Not for an instant would I question his sincerity, but there is no way he could possibly have understood the depth of truth in the statement he had just uttered. Many people do not realize that for the first twenty-seven years of our marriage I did not provide my wife with any real financial security. Now that does not mean we were always broke, but we were on a financial roller coaster most of the time. For example, in one five-year stretch I was involved in seventeen different ventures. I tried every "get rich quick" deal that came down the pike until I finally got so broke I had to go to work.

During all those years I don't once remember The Redhead saying, "If we just had more money, we could. . . ." It was always, "You can do it, Honey; tomorrow will be better." Ladies, there is no way I could begin to tell you what it meant to me to have a cheerleader cheering me on every day and praying for me every night. Gentlemen, there is no way I can describe to you the impact it will have on your wife and your relationship with her if you become her cheerleader and number one booster. To believe in, encourage, and support her will make an enormous difference. God designed us to function as a team, and teams do better, much better, than two individuals.

STABLE MARRIAGES FOR PERSONAL AND CAREER SUCCESS_____

Evidence is overwhelming that a good marriage gives the individuals involved an infinitely better chance of being successful in their careers and personal lives. This is not to imply that those who are not in stable marriages cannot achieve these objectives, but the evidence is clear that a good marriage is a marvelous base from which to build a more successful personal life and business career.

There is a prevailing myth that you can't be a hard-charging, successful businessman or businesswoman and be a good spouse and parent at the same time, but the evidence is solid that the word *myth* is applicable and appropriate!

Four independent studies all proved that highly paid (one study included 1,139 CEO's with an average annual income of $356,000) and successful (all studies included "executive level only") men and women had some similar qualities:

1. *Loyalty to their spouse*. Most were married over twenty-five years, and many were still married to their high-school or college sweetheart.
2. *A commitment to family*. Eight out of ten had two, three, four, or more children, and nine out of ten claimed their families to be their first priority.
3. *A religious affiliation*. The majority of the thousands of participants regularly attended church or synagogue.
4. *A balanced life-style*. Nine of ten exercise regularly, don't smoke, have a reasonable amount of leisure time, and get an adequate amount of sleep. Interestingly enough, their work week fits into the fifty- to fifty-five-hour category—long hours, but by no means workaholic hours.
5. *A true love for people*. This concern begins at home with the spouse and children. The majority of the

truly effective and successful executives spend any and all free time with their families.

When you think about it for a moment, it certainly makes sense that if people can establish a loving and compatible relationship at home, they have a better chance of establishing winning relationships with those with whom they work on a regular basis. Realistically you simply can't separate your personal, family, and business lives. You might not discuss your personal and family problems with your associates on the job, but you take those problems with you and they *do* affect your performance.

The extent of that effect was revealed in a study reported in the January 8, 1990, *USA Today*, which stated that marital problems including divorce have a bigger impact on productivity than alcohol or drug abuse. Forty-two percent of those surveyed call the impact of marital problems "very negative," 27 percent feel that way about alcohol abuse and 22 percent about drug abuse.

Yes, it's true that a stable family environment is a marvelous place for career success to begin. A beautiful relationship with your mate will enhance your creativity and upgrade your standard of living while improving your quality of life.

I AM AN OPTIMIST

Most people who know me either personally or through my books, tapes, and seminars would identify me as an optimist. As you probably know, an optimist is a person who, when he wears his shoes out, just figures he's back on his feet! As an optimist, I often tell people that I'm just a few years past middle age. This surprises many of them because they know that I'm over seventy. Then I explain that since I'm going to live to be a hundred and twenty, I'm obviously slightly past middle age.

Yes, I know I'm not promised or guaranteed fifty-seven more seconds much less fifty-seven more years. However, the fact that I am married increases my odds of living longer. Married men ages twenty-five to forty-four have a death rate less than half as high as that of unmarried men. Among women, the mortality rate for single women is almost double that of married women.

Even the Greek philosopher Socrates was promarriage. He is said to have told his students, "By all means, marry. If you get a good wife, you will become very happy. If you get a bad one, you will become a philosopher—and that is also good." Marriage may not mean living happily ever after, but it does mean living *happier* and longer.

With those thoughts in mind, let me say I am enormously optimistic about marriage in general, and *yours* and mine in particular. I hasten to add that my thinking is not a blind, pie-in-the-sky optimism, but an optimism based on more than forty-three years of an extremely happy marriage. In your case, I believe that if your marriage is not the greatest at the moment, it has potential for stabilizing and even developing into a twentieth-century love story. Sometimes all that is needed is a change of heart and attitude. My own marriage has not been good 100 percent of the time. As a matter of fact, we've had some tough times, but I can tell you that as the years go by, our love and relationship grow and we love each other more and enjoy each other more than ever before.

In your marriage, I strongly believe that the seeds of success are already present but, realistically, so are the seeds of failure. The choice really boils down to which seeds you are going to feed, water, and cultivate. In most cases, beautiful marriages are the result of a long series of right choices you've made along the way, and miserable marriages are the result of a long series of poor choices you've made. My natural optimism, combined with the fact that you've read this far, tells me that you are vitally interested in making the choices you need to make in order for your marriage to grow into the loving one it's capable of becoming.

A *REAL LOVE STORY*

Within the bonds of holy matrimony, the possibility of *real* love exists. I shall never forget witnessing one of the most real and sincere love stories of all time. I was in South Alabama visiting with my brother, Huie Ziglar. His wife, Jewell, had been in Michigan City, Indiana, with their daughter for the birth of their first grandchild. I was seated on the front porch that summer afternoon. My brother was in the kitchen when his son returned from picking up Jewell at the bus station. They drove into the front yard, and when my brother heard the car door close, he immediately ran from the kitchen to the front yard. By the time he arrived, Jewell was out of the car. They hugged, kissed, and wept like babies as they promised each other that never again would they be separated for any reason.

As I viewed this tender scene between this little country preacher and his bride of thirty-three years, I could not help but wonder what it would be like if the television cameras of the world had been turned on this *real* love story—a love story based on mutual love, respect, putting the other one first, and sacrifice during all their years together. She had borne him six wonderful children: five fine sons and a beautiful daughter. She had nursed them through sickness, made most of their clothes, kept a clean house, prepared all the meals, and been a faithful and loving wife to her husband all of those years.

For his part, he had given her his all—all of his affection, all of his devotion, all of his loyalty. My brother's income as a country preacher was not nearly enough to support the family, so he had a little farm where he raised their fruits and vegetables. He also had cows, chickens, and hogs that provided food and a small income. Huie and Jewell often reached the end of their financial rope and then simply tied a knot and held on! Materially speaking, they never had very much, but I can tell you I've never been in a home where there was as much love and laughter as in that home. Husband and wife were extremely close; parents and children were extremely close. How marvelous it would be if America's children saw love stories like that on a daily basis so they would have some real role models for direction and guidance!

In *Courtship After Marriage*, I am going to share some ideas and specific action steps on how you and your spouse can capture (or recapture) the deep and true love my brother and sister-in-love shared.

You can't saw sawdust.

NO GUILT TRIP, PLEASE

Before we close the door on this first chapter, I would like to emphasize that if you have had a failed marriage or you are having family difficulties, my intention is not to hang any feelings of guilt on you. The past is exactly that—the past. You can't saw sawdust, and what is done is done. If you put this book down thinking or feeling that if you had just taken "such and such" actions your family would still be together, I will have failed in a major objective of the book.

Chances are excellent that any mistakes you've made have been mistakes of the head and not of the heart. Like most people, you did *what you did when you did it* because at the time and under those circumstances, *with the information you had available*, that *was the best you could have done—* period. Let's leave it at that. Nothing will be accomplished by whipping yourself at this stage of the game. The pages of your past cannot be rewritten, but the pages of your tomorrows are blank. Let's work together to fill them properly, joyously, and positively. I personally hope—and yes, I believe—the best is yet to come. So if we can increase joy and happiness for the present and prevent grief and heartache for the future, this book will have accomplished its objective—and then some.

2 | I MARRIED THE WRONG PERSON

Marriages may be made in heaven, but a lot of the details have to be worked out here on earth.
—Gloria Pitzer

A Roman Catholic girl was dating a Southern Baptist boy, and after their fifth date, the girl's mom could tell her daughter was really motivated about this guy. So she sat her down for a serious woman-to-woman talk.

Going straight to the point, she said, "Now, daughter, you know us Catholics don't marry those Baptists. And those Baptists don't marry us Catholics. You're going to have to terminate this relationship."

The daughter replied, "Mom, it's too late. I've already fallen in love with him. Can't we do something?" Seeing the hurt and disappointment in her daughter's eyes, she thought for a moment and said, "Sure, we'll just sell this boy on taking catechism classes and make a good Catholic out of him. Then you can get married."

They started the sales process, and it was an easy sale. In fact, the boy was already sold on the real product—the girl. So the boy took catechism, the wedding plans were set, the announcements sent out, the church reserved, gifts began coming in. Everybody was gung ho.

Then about a week before the wedding, the young lady came in from an evening out with her beloved, great big tears pouring from her eyes, saying, "Mom, it's all over. Call the priest. Cancel the wedding. Call the guests. Send back the gifts."

The stunned mother said, "Wait a minute. I don't understand. What's the matter? I thought we sold that boy on being a good Catholic."

The daughter tearfully replied, "Mom, that's the problem. We've oversold. He's going to be a priest."

The reality is, many couples, when they are courting, do oversell. In essence, they do not, at least initially, reveal exactly who they are, how they think, and what they believe. That's one of the prime reasons the courtship process should be fairly lengthy. Yes, I know we all have heard stories of how Bill and Sally met on Tuesday and three weeks later were walking down the aisle and forty years later were still living in wedded bliss, but those stories are few and far between.

THE ULTIMATE DECEIVER

The difficulty often starts when the honeymoon is over and Prince Charming turns out to be less than he said he was, and Cinderella doesn't quite measure up to her press clippings. In short, you come to the inescapable conclusion that you have married the wrong person, or at least you did not marry the person you *thought* you were marrying. The reason you reach this inescapable conclusion after four whole weeks of marriage, according to psychologist Charles Lowery, is obvious: Of all the people on the face of the earth, surely the ultimate deceiver is the person seriously involved in the courtship process with marriage in mind. Not only do such people put their best foot forward, but they shine it up and keep it forward throughout the entire process. That's one of the reasons wise courters will have a two-year waiting period before they get married. Psychiatrist Ross Campbell says it takes about that long to reveal an entire character, and even two years is sometimes rushing the issue.

Now, what's this about being the ultimate deceiver during the courtship process? Let's listen in on some courtship conversations and see if any of you married folks recognize some of these comments:

HE: Aw, Honey, I just love to go shopping! No, I don't mind waiting while you try on a few dresses. As a matter of fact, I'm flattered that you want me to express an opinion on what looks best on you!

Or

Your mom is such a delightful lady! Talks too much? My goodness, no! I think her conversation is witty, and she certainly has some marvelous insights on how I should dress and how I can get ahead in my career.

Or

No, no, I was not the least bit offended when your dad monopolized the conversation. I really do enjoy war stories, and after all, I can eat and listen at the same time.

SHE: Sure, Honey, I love the great outdoors! Not only would I be delighted to ride the golf cart with you and watch you play, but I certainly plan on learning so you and I can play together. It will be wonderful to know we can still be playing together well up into the twilight years of our life, and even raise our children to join us on the course.

Or

No, no, Honey, I don't mind cold weather at all! I'll be happy to join you for the football games, and certainly a little ice and snow, on occasion, would be invigorating. After all, we do have warm clothes to wear.

Or

Actually, I'm an early riser and it's certainly no big deal to get up at three o'clock in the morning and drive 150 miles to be in the deer stand an hour before the deer start moving around.

Or

Actually, your mother *is* the best cook I've ever seen,

and she certainly has some marvelous ideas on raising children. After all, look what a marvelous job she
did with you.

FROM COURTSHIP TO CRITICISM

In some shape, form, or fashion, some of the above does
happen. Before marriage, we are on our best behavior. The
sales process is going full speed ahead because we are enam-
ored of the other person and convinced in our own minds
that he or she is the right one. "After all, there were too
many unusual circumstances for our meeting to be coinci-
dental. Surely, no one would believe it's just chance that he
came from the biggest city in America and I came from the
smallest. Surely, it's more than ironic that he loves the same
type restaurant I do, and it can't just be a quirk of fate that
we both come from large families. And it can't be a coinci-
dence that we both enjoy reading, we were both the second
children in our families, and both of us finished in the part
of the class that makes the top half possible!"

Yes, it's amazing how, when we start looking, we can
find all kinds of justifications for knowing that this really is a
match made in heaven. It's even more amazing, however,
that when the honeymoon ends, we suddenly discover that
the very reasons we were initially attracted become the very
reasons we can't get along. He was the strong, silent type,
but now he is labeled "uncommunicative." She was full of
personality, open friendliness, and new ideas, but now she is
superficial, flirtatious, and shallow.

Often, time does either change things or open our eyes.
But experience in picking a mate is certainly no guarantee
we'll get better with practice. Roughly 50 percent of all first
marriages now end in divorce. About 60 percent of all second marriages, 70 percent of all third marriages, and over
80 percent of all fourth marriages also end in divorce. So, as

a matter of fact, statistics prove we make the best choice in a partner *the first time!* The question, then, is a relatively simple one: What can we do to improve our relationship with the one we have, turn that marriage around so that our relationship with the one we promised to love and cherish forever not only becomes meaningful and exciting, but gets better as the years go by? (Or what can you do if you are currently on your second or even third or fourth marriage so that you become a "stat buster" and make this marriage a magnificent one?)

START HERE

A good place to start is with this advice given to us by Mrs. Ruth Stafford Peale in *Plus—The Magazine of Positive Thinking*. She writes the advice to young wives: "Study your man. Study him as if he were some rare, strange and fascinating animal. Study him constantly because he will be constantly changing. Study his likes and dislikes, his strengths and weaknesses, his moods and mannerisms. Just loving a man is fine, but it's not enough. To live with one successfully you have to know him. And to know him, you have to study him."

Surely no one would question the wisdom of that advice from Mrs. Peale. Now let me be bold enough to give some advice to young husbands as well as middle-aged and older ones: "Study your woman. Study her as if she were some rare, strange and fascinating animal. Study her constantly because she will be constantly changing. Study her likes and dislikes, her strengths and weaknesses, her moods and mannerisms. Just loving a woman is fine, but it's not enough. To live with one successfully you have to know her. And to know her, you have to study her."

The reasoning is crystal clear. If you did "marry the wrong person" or at least married someone different from the one you thought you were marrying, then you obviously do not know the person you did marry. I'm sure you will agree that the first step to getting along with this "stranger" is to learn as much as you can . . . so *study* him or her very carefully.

YOU WON'T CHANGE YOUR SPOUSE _____

In our survey of the couples who had been married twenty-five years or more and who would marry the same person again, we discovered that an overwhelming majority (84 percent) of them took their mates not only for better or worse but *as they are*. Eighty-nine percent of them, after all their years together, claimed to "strive to accept" their mates just the way they are right now. When asked what they would change about their mates if they had the opportunity, one woman simply said, "After twenty-five years—nothing." One husband said, "Only her health." Some pointed to relatively small areas of change such as, "his driving habits," "more help with the housework," "posture," or "waiting 'til the last minute to get ready to go." Of those who did go into marriage thinking they might change their mates (16 percent), they were perhaps best represented by the lady who said, "I thought I could 'mellow' his ways with lots of love and T.L.C."

Apparently these husbands and wives who are *happily married* recognize the wisdom of accepting their mates as they are and the futility of seeking perfection and trying to change them. So your question is, "That's good for them, but my marriage is not so hot, so what can I do to make mine better?" Good question. And the answer is:

YOU *START* BY CHANGING YOU _____

Your first step is to find out exactly where you are at this stage of your courtship with your mate. To help you do this, Don Hawkins and his associates have designed a courtship quiz that is the most logical and comprehensive I've seen. I *strongly* encourage you to get a pencil (so you can erase) or a pen and a separate sheet of paper to score your answers. *Make this the most serious quiz you have ever taken.* Then take the quiz and answer the questions from your perspective; next, answer them as to how you think your mate will respond. When you have finished, encourage your mate to do exactly what you just did. Then compare notes.

For many (if not most) couples, this will truly be an eye-opener. You will probably discover that your marriage is not quite where you thought it was or where your mate thought it was. You *will* discover where your marriage *is*. I firmly believe that this information will throw the communication doors wide open; and with the rest of the information in this book (which I strongly encourage *both* of you to read, study and, most important, *discuss*) I believe you can make a bad relationship much, much better and a good relationship magnificent. Try it; the marriage you improve (maybe even save) will be your own.

THE STATE OF YOUR COURTSHIP QUIZ _____

Please mark your answers, then see the scoring details on page 43.

1. We hold hands . . . (a) several times a day, especially when walking or in public; (b) two or three times a week—whether we need to or not; (c) occasionally—but not usually; (d) never or almost never.
2. I am able to share with my spouse . . . (a) the good and the bad of each day—and both of us enjoy the sharing; (b) the good things that happen, but usually not the bad; (c) once or twice a week—but usually we're just too busy; (d) very little of what happens in my life—it's just too volatile and not worth the risk.
3. We talk about . . . (a) what's happening in our lives and how we feel about things; (b) the events of life—but we

have to be very careful about sharing feelings, it's risky; (c) some things, but quite a few areas are out of bounds in terms of our talking about them; (d) just the basics— the kids, the car, the schedule, the budget.

4. Our physical or sexual relationship is . . . (a) excellent—in fact it's better than when we first married; (b) regular and pretty satisfying—but seldom dramatic; (c) "hit or miss"; (d) almost more trouble than it's worth.

5. In our relationship, romance . . . (a) isn't just tied to sex, but is an integral part of every day—a touch of the hand, a shared look across the room, a special gift for no occasion; (b) is part of most occasions when we make love, but usually not at other times; (c) usually blooms on special occasions such as Valentine's, anniversary, etc.; (d) seems to have gone the way of the nickel candy bar.

6. In our marriage, money is . . . (a) a subject we handle as a partnership; (b) a subject we try to avoid; (c) a source of occasional conflict; (d) the trigger for ongoing marital war.

7. In our marriage, most decisions, especially major ones, are made . . . (a) jointly, after thorough discussion; (b) usually by just one of us; (c) only after the trauma of a major conflict; (d) only after postponement due to war—and sometimes not at all.

8. We handle conflict . . . (a) by facing it—and each other— head-on; lovingly sharing feelings, listening to each other, perhaps even holding hands while we're having the discussion, then "making up"; (b) by ignoring it mostly—we have very little conflict—but the exceptions can be explosive and deadly; (c) pretty well occasionally—but some topics produce a lot of bloodshed, name calling, and "low blows"; (d) very poorly—we dredge up the past, call names, inflict a lot of pain and threats, even though we should be good at this since we argue a lot.

9. We go out on dates . . . (a) regularly, at least weekly, and

we enjoy them; (b) once or twice a month—and usually we have a good time; (c) occasionally—and sometimes we even enjoy them; (d) not at all—isn't dating for unmarried people?

10. My view of marriage is . . . (a) a lifelong commitment, a shared partnership, the best relationship possible between two humans; (b) the same as "(a)" officially, but we occasionally threaten or discuss wanting to be out of the marriage; (c) like that of my spouse—we both seem to feel we're not "quite right" for each other, but we'll probably stick it out; (d) if the marriage survives, it may take a miracle.

11. My spouse is . . . (a) my best friend, my lover and only romantic interest, and my life partner; (b) two of the above (you pick 'em); (c) one of the above; (d) none of the above—but at least we're still together, even if only by a thread.

12. Our marriage relationship . . . (a) takes work, but it's worth it—the rewards far exceed the cost of the effort; (b) has been pretty easy, but at times I feel we need to work harder; (c) often seems it isn't quite worth the effort it takes; (d) doesn't get much effort anymore.

13. My spouse accepts me . . . (a) unconditionally, with genuine acceptance and love, flaws and all—just as I am; (b) most of the time, but he/she would sure like to change a few things; (c) as is, but also as a "project" because he/she is constantly letting me know how I need to improve; (d) did you say accepts . . . I feel I'm given the ultimatum, "improve or else!"

14. I accept my spouse . . . (a) unconditionally, good and bad, strengths and flaws; (b) pretty much, but there are some needed changes; (c) to a degree, but I'm trying to get those changes made; (d) I've come close to giving up on trying to change him/her—the accepting part I gave up on a long time ago.

15. Spiritually, we . . . (a) are right together in our commit-

ment to a shared personal faith in God; (b) both have a strong faith, but we disagree on some key issues; (c) have little interest—and that seems to be O.K. with both of us most of the time; (d) seem to be at war over spiritual issues a lot of the time.

16. When it comes to areas of disagreement, such as how strict to be with the kids or whether to make a major purchase, we . . . (a) discuss all sides and possibilities, then agree on a resolution; (b) decide who will give in (usually me—usually him/her); in other words, one of us rules the roost; (c) move from discussion to major conflict—often without successful resolution—or one of us just withdraws; (d) add the question to our list of "battle issues" in our ongoing marital conflict.

17. Being away from each other, even briefly as on an overnight business trip, . . . (a) constitutes a hard-to-endure time during which we both look forward eagerly to reunion—and we really do enjoy "the reunion"; (b) is something we've become more used to over time—but we still really miss each other; (c) constitutes something that can give us some relief from conflict, hassles, etc.; (d) has come to be viewed as a high point in our "existence."

18. If I had my choice . . . (a) my spouse and I would spend an extended time together on a trip to some special enjoyable place; (b) we'd do a short trip together—we seem to become bored with each other if it's just the two of us for too long; (c) we wouldn't go anywhere together—it's not worth the hassles, besides there are too many responsibilities at home; (d) I'd take an extended trip to Tahiti—without my spouse.

19. Weekend or overnight "romantic" getaways are . . . (a) regular items—scheduled—and sources of great enjoyment; (b) occasional treats—wish they could be more often; (c) items we feature much less on our schedule

than we used to; (d) part of our past—if we ever included them.

20. Our other friendships (with couples, individuals, etc.) . . . (a) never precede our relationship with each other, but they actually seem to strengthen and enhance our relationship; (b) can either help us or, as sometimes happens, detract from our relationship; (c) are non-existent—we have no other friends, just the two of us; (d) are a source of continual problems and conflicts.

SCORING: To determine the status of the Courtship Factor in your marriage, give yourself 5 points for every (a), 3 points for every (b), 1 point for every (c), and zero for every (d) answer. Then go back and add up this "semiscientific" quiz to find out where you rated.

80–100	You're courting—keep up the good work.
60–80	You need a "courtship tune-up."
40–60	I recommend you start courting—and fast. Perhaps this book will help.
Less than 40	You probably need more than just this book. I'd recommend a marriage therapist, pronto.

THINK ABOUT THIS_____

Think back on the examples shared earlier of how courting couples "deceive" each other. I will confess that there's a certain amount of "stretch" in the scenarios. However, there is far more truth than stretch, and there are also two tremendous lessons we can learn from these illustrations that will make our lives richer and our marriage infinitely better.

   1. In the courtship process each party went overboard to please the other one. Each indicated a willingness, even an eagerness, to do things with the other one that were of no personal interest. Each did that to please the other person and to share the moment. Obviously, this can be overdone, but in the real world, doing things with your mate strictly because you want to please him or her and spend time together helps build relationships. Over a period of time, the effectiveness of this approach will be validated in the strengthening of your marriage.

There's also an excellent chance that in the process of "going along with your mate," you just might develop an interest in the things your mate so thoroughly enjoys.

Classic example: My love for golf is well known, but The Redhead was considerably less than enthusiastic about the game until several years ago when out of the blue she announced that she was going to "give golf another chance." (She had given it a short-term try years earlier.) Since I had just received a two-hundred-dollar gift certificate for participating in a charity golf tournament, I invested that money (and some more, too) to get her some clubs. Next, she took a couple of lessons from a laid-back pro who really knew how to teach beginners. Result: First time out she hit several good shots and really enjoyed playing. Today, she loves the game and from time to time even plays with our son when I'm out of town. The highlight of her golf career, thus far, occurred the last time we played (as of this writing), when she beat me the first nine holes. Needless to say, this event has not gone unmentioned among our friends, relatives, club members, associates, and complete strangers.

Bottom line: She decided to play almost entirely to please me. I was delighted because her decision meant I could play the game I love with the one I love. Now, she loves the game nearly as much as I do, so we have something else in common, which brings us even closer than we were before. Our often-quoted philosophy, "You can have everything in life you want if you will just help enough other people get what they want," is certainly applicable here.

2. *During the premarriage courtship, we looked for and told others about the good qualities of our future mate.* Being patient, understanding, pleasant, and agreeable while finding good things to say about your future mate (and your future in-loves) is excellent training for the future of the marriage. Despite what you might have heard, you do marry the whole family, so your ability to get along with your mate's parents could well be the determining factor in both the longevity and the happiness of the marriage. In addition, having patience and understanding and being pleasant and agreeable are qualities that will build a good marriage.

Looking for the good in your mate and your mate's family not only enhances your relationship at home, it gives you some marvelous experience for getting ahead in your career as well.

BE A "GOOD" FINDER

Andrew Carnegie said, "No man can become rich without himself enriching others." He went on to live this philosophy, as evidenced by the forty-three millionaires he had working for him. A reporter interviewing Mr. Carnegie asked how he was able to hire that many millionaires. Mr. Carnegie patiently explained that the men were not million-

> ## Look for the gold—look for the good in your mate.

aires when they came to work for him but had become millionaires *by* working for him. The reporter pursued the line of questioning. How did Mr. Carnegie develop these men to become so valuable? How was he able to pay them so much that they became millionaires? Mr. Carnegie replied, "You develop people in the same way you mine for gold. When you mine for gold, you must literally move tons of dirt to find a single ounce of gold. However, you do not look for the dirt—you look for the gold."

Looking for the gold (the good) in others is not only a sound idea in business, it's an even better one in marriage as this next example illustrates. Incidentally, I know there are some who will read this story and think it's nothing but a fairy tale, but I can emphatically assure you that the story of "Johnny Lingo" is much more than fantasy.

WANTED: ONE TEN-COW WIFE _____

Many years ago, on the island of Oahu in the Hawaiian Islands, the people observed a most unusual custom. A prospective husband paid a family a certain number of cows for their daughter to become his wife. The standard price was three cows for a bride. If she was an unusual catch, with all the beauty and attributes one would want in a wife, there were a few instances where a bride fetched four cows. There was a rumor, though it was unconfirmed, that at some time in the distant past, in one of the more remote areas of the island, one young damsel with truly unusual charm, beauty, and character had gone for the astronomical price of five cows.

On the island lived a man with two daughters. The older one was what we would term, in our society, a "reject" or a "loser." She was the "runt of the litter." Her father had despaired of ever getting three cows for her and had long ago determined that he would gladly accept a two-cow offer, and if the suitor was a good bargainer, he had already decided he would let her go for one cow. The truth is, if push came to shove, in order to rid himself of the burden of having to feed her all her life, old Dad would have gladly let her go for no cows. That was not so with her younger sister, a ravishing beauty with charm and character, so old Dad knew he would easily rid himself of her and was not concerned in the least about her future.

When Johnny Lingo,* the richest man on the island, came calling on this household, everyone knew he was coming to see the younger daughter. To everyone's astonishment—and to Dad's delight—he came calling on the older daughter. Old Dad just about flipped with joy! Since Johnny was the richest man as well as the most generous on the island, old Dad knew that Johnny would, in his generosity, be delighted to give at least the standard three-cow price. He even let his imagination get the better of him and thought that since Johnny was both generous and wealthy, he might even go four cows. Then his imagination turned to insanity, and he figured maybe Johnny would even go for the rumored price of five cows. You can imagine his delight when Johnny came to claim his bride and brought *ten* cows with him! Old Dad almost had a heart attack! He quickly called the tribal chief to perform the ceremony before Johnny changed his mind, died suddenly, or regained his senses.

NOW HERE'S A HONEYMOON

In those days a standard honeymoon lasted one year, but when you have a ten-cow bride, you obviously do not take a standard three-cow honeymoon. So bride and groom set off for parts unknown with the announced intention of a full two-year honeymoon. When the day arrived for the return of the bride and groom, a lookout was posted on the edge of the village with instructions to sound the call as Johnny and his bride first came into sight.

---

*From Aubrey P. Andelin *Man of Steel and Velvet* (Santa Barbara, Calif.: Pacific Press, 1972).

Shortly after daylight the call was sounded: "Here comes a couple!" Naturally, the query was, "Is it the bride and groom?" He answered that he thought so, but he wasn't certain. He recognized Johnny immediately, but he wasn't sure about the girl. Something about her was familiar, and yet, she was strikingly beautiful—graceful, poised, confident, and self-assured. When the couple drew closer, they could see she was truly the same girl. However, she had changed dramatically. Her beauty, charm, competent bearing, and poise were obvious even to the most casual observer. And those who looked closely thought Johnny Lingo had gotten a bargain by paying "only" ten cows.

I recognize the fact the some of you who read this might dismiss it as legend, but the reality is that the Johnny Lingo story has happened not once in the long ago on a distant island, but thousands of times all over the world on a regular basis. Think of what Johnny's action did for his bride's confidence, self-image, frame of mind, and every other positive asset. The reality is that the instant Johnny paid the ten cows, she became a ten-cow wife—and it happens all the time.

Gentlemen, if you want a ten-cow wife, you should start treating her like a ten-cow wife. Not only that, fellows, but if you'll treat her like a thoroughbred, you'll never end up with a nag. Ladies, it works the same way for your husbands (actually it works better). Man doesn't live by bread alone; he needs to be "buttered up" from time to time. Treat him like a "champ," and you'll never end up with a "chump"!

Goethe expressed it this way: "If you treat a man as he is, he will stay as he is. If you treat him as if he were what he ought to be and could be, he will become that bigger and better man." Message: Give your mate something to live *up* to, not *down* to, and you will end up with a "better" mate, which is the key to a better marriage.

3 | I'LL JUST GET A DIVORCE

Partnership must precede parenthood. A man is a
husband first, father second, businessman third.
A woman is a wife first, mother second, career
woman third. A strong marriage precedes a strong
family. Marriage is permanent; parenthood is
temporary. Marriage is central; parenthood is
secondary. Marriage is the hub; children are the
spokes. The child-centered home is poor training
for the child, poor marriage insurance, poor
preparation for the empty nest. Your partner is
first, before children, job or career. A man must
love his wife as himself, and the wife must honor
her husband (Ephesians 5:33).

—Dr. J. Allan Petersen

A little guy was confronted by three bullies, any one of
whom could have obliterated him, and they were giving some evidence that they had that plan in mind. The little
guy was very bright, so he backed away from the three bullies, drew a line in the dirt, backed up a few more steps,
looked into the eyes of the biggest of the three, and said,
"Now, you just step across that line." Confidently, the big
bully did exactly that, and the little guy just grinned and
said, "Now, we're both on the same side."

YOU *ARE* ON THE SAME SIDE

Surely any marriage that's going to avoid divorce must
have husbands and wives who clearly understand that they
really are on the same side. For the marriage to survive, husband and wife must be friends, and the dictionary says that
a *friend* is a close acquaintance, a supporter, and "one at-
tached to another by esteem, respect and affection, an inti-

49

mate, a person on the same side in a struggle." Most husbands and wives, even in the most beautiful of marriages, will still tell you that marriage is a struggle.

ROMANTIC—BUT WRONG

My friend, Dr. Richard Furman, whom I will mention quite often in this book, tells the story of the high-school quarterback who had fallen in love with one of the cheerleaders and the romance was quite serious. He graduated a year ahead of her and went off to college. They kept in close contact via phone calls and through the mail. As Christmas neared, he wrote her a letter telling her he was coming home. Would she meet him at nine o'clock on Friday night on the fifty-yard line in the football stadium?

The symbolism was obvious: They were going to be meeting each other halfway, and while the romanticists might approve of the creativity of the young man, those who've been involved in marriage counseling and a happy relationship with a mate instantly recognize the fact that marriage is not a 50/50 proposition. It is purely and simply a 100/100 proposition. The husband goes 100 percent of the way to please his wife, love her totally, commit himself completely and stand faithfully by her side. The wife makes identical commitments. That really is the only way the marriage can be completely successful.

VERY IMPORTANT!

If you are divorced and are thinking, "I am a failure," let me state emphatically: _Failure is an event, not a person._ All of us feel the impact of divorce. I have personally observed the horrors of divorce in friends and family, so I want to make one point very clear. This chapter is _not_ for people going through a divorce or those who have just been divorced. You already have experienced what I am writing about. "Rehashing" old hurts would only be painful, and there is no need to pour "salt in the wound." (In other words, move directly to chapter 4.)

The purpose of this chapter is not to "whip up" on people who are divorced and put them on a guilt trip. The benefits from that approach would be minus zero. This chapter is written for people whose marriage is in trouble and who think of divorce as the lesser of two evils. If you are considering, have considered, or will ever consider divorce, read on . . . but get ready because you are about to face the facts with no "sugarcoating."

IS DIVORCE THAT MUCH OF A PROBLEM?_____

If you are married today, divorce is a PROBABILITY more than a POSSIBILITY. Think with me as I explain that somewhat startling statement. Divorce rates have risen more than 700 percent over the last fifty years, and the number of single-parent families has mushroomed. For example, in 1948 only one out of fourteen children under the age of six was brought up by a single parent. By 1973, that proportion was one out of seven. Today, that statistic is one out of five. Divorces worldwide are highest for childless or single-child couples between the ages of twenty-five and twenty-nine. Divorce data tabulated for fifty-eight countries, regions, and cultures between 1947 and 1981 showed the so-called seven-year itch was actually a four-year itch and most marriages that will end in divorce will break up by the fourth year. In the United States, marriages are more likely to end by the second year. That's tragic.

This rising divorce rate is probably one reason many publications have changed focus from how to have an ideal marriage to how to get a painless divorce. One society band leader whose orchestras have played for some ten thousand weddings instructs his musicians, "Always play your best. Men, remember a lot of these brides will be getting married again." He's clearly implying that maybe they can play for the same bride again because 45 percent of all marriages are remarriages. I recently read about a lawyer who offers a drive-up window for persons seeking information on divorce. The attitude our society has developed toward divorce is devastating.

PIE CRUST PROMISES

I came across a comic strip recently in which one character said, "You know, it's odd, but now that I'm actually engaged, I'm starting to feel nervous about getting married!"

The other character replied, "I know what you're thinking. It's only natural to be nervous! After all, marriage is a big commitment—seven or eight years can be a long time!"

Another cartoon I saw pictured a young fellow and his girlfriend at the jewelry store checking out engagement rings. Turning to his beloved, the young man says, "Let's get a little one, Honey. After all this is just the first marriage for both of us."

What's going on here is something we might call a pie crust promises approach to marriage. Now if you're familiar with the film *Mary Poppins*, you'll know what I'm talking about. After their incredible first day with the amazing Mary Poppins, the two children, Jane and Michael Banks, jumped into bed. Jane asked, "Mary Poppins, you won't ever leave us, will you?" Full of excitement, Michael looked at his new nanny and added, "Will you stay if we promise to be good?"

As Mary tucked the two children in, she replied, "Look, that's a pie crust promise. Easily made, easily broken!"

In today's world, a lot of men and women have gone to the altar before a judge or even a minister and made lots of pie crust promises, which they broke at the first sign of trouble. The reality is that many couples spend more time planning their wedding than they do their marriage.

FACING THE ISSUE

I believe that being informed is a more realistic approach to life than blindly going along hoping "things will work out." I share the realities of divorce with you so you can make a better decision as it relates to your own life as well as the lives of your mate and children.

Let's take a close look at you and nine of your married friends who choose divorce. Now I'm not talking about someone "walking out" on you (although psychologists confirm that everyone who "chooses" to walk out feels forced to make that choice as a last alternative). When you choose divorce, after two years, seven of the ten members of your group will seriously consider their divorce a mistake, and five of the group will have gone through a second divorce. The majority of the people will still be angry and bitter toward the spouse, which will have a negative impact on the relationships with their children. And hear this: Only one person in your group will even CLAIM to have a happy and satisfying life ten years later. Still convinced you will beat the odds and be the *one?* Then read on.

The economic consequences of divorce are devastating. Almost half of those women who don't remarry will be on welfare (compared with one of ten two-parent households). Only half the fathers who divorce will see their children regularly. The standard of living for women and their children will drop substantially. For every ten dollars spent the year *before* the divorce, you will have three dollars to spend *after* the divorce. Half of you fathers will fail to support your children, and almost that many will not even see the children for twelve months.

A question for dad: If you knew *your* child's standard of living would drop 73 percent and you wouldn't see him for the next year, would you still go through with the divorce (if it's your choice), or would you take every conceivable step to save the marriage?

A question for mom: If you knew that your children and you were going to suffer in an incredible manner mentally and financially and that your chances for happiness in the near (and distant) future were minimal at best, would you still go through with the divorce (if it's your choice), or would you take every conceivable step to save the marriage?

In these days of "disposable marriage," treating divorce as "morally neutral—an option no better or worse than staying married"—is irreparably damaging to the very people who need help.

WHAT CHOICE DO I HAVE?

The therapists with whom I've talked and whose works I have studied say that instead of changing mates, couples should first consider changing themselves. Unhealthy marriages are born out of unhealthy emotional needs. And these needs must be met and changed individually for a couple to have a happy marriage. Those individuals who feel that the answer is to divorce and look for another mate usually end up marrying a mate with the same emotional needs. The real answer to unhealthy emotional situations is not pursuing a new mate, but pursuing both individual and marriage

> **"Divorce is second only to the death of a spouse in terms of emotional impact."**
> **—Frank Minirth**

therapy to learn how to get those personal emotional needs met in appropriate ways.

According to my friend, psychiatrist Frank Minirth, whose Minirth-Meier Clinics treat thousands of individuals from across America for depression and other mental health disorders, "divorce is second only to the death of a spouse in terms of emotional impact." Dr. Minirth believes the ultimate negative emotional results of divorce are even greater than losing a mate through death. He points out that when you lose a mate in death, you have no choice. However, in most cases, divorce is a choice.

WHO LOSES?

The real victims of divorce in many cases are the children. I believe that many parents have no real idea (or don't stop to think about) what impact the divorce has on the children. I can tell you from close observation of my own family as well as families in our church, in our company, and in society in general, that the impact on most children is very negative. This has nothing to do with who's right or wrong and is certainly not an attack on the integrity of either the husband or the wife. The fact is, even under "ideal" circumstances the children of divorce generally suffer.

> **"The best thing a parent can do for a child is to love his or her spouse."**
> **—Zig Ziglar**

Many people who are contemplating divorce don't realize the truth of what psychologists have pointed out—that the most important thing a father can do for his children is to love their mother and the most important thing a mother can do for her children is to love their father. This reality was brought home to me one day when my son was about fifteen years old. We were taking a walk and holding a serious father-to-son conversation. I asked him, "Son, if anyone should ask you what you liked best about your dad, what would you say?"

He paused for a moment and said, "I'd say that the thing I like best about my dad is that he loves my mom." Naturally I asked, "Son, why would you say that?" He replied, "I know because you love Mom you're going to treat her right, and as long as you treat her right, we will always be a family, because I know how much Mom loves you." Then he said some words that verbalize the feelings of children all over America, "That means, Dad, that I will never have to choose between you and Mom."

I had no way of knowing it at that point, but that very day one of his closest friends had been given the choice of living with mom or dad.

RESULTS: PAINFUL AND LONG LASTING

Ten million children in America have watched their parents divorce, and that number is growing by one million each year. Since we looked at your options when choosing divorce, let's look at the results for those who have very few options: the children involved. Almost half of the children will enter adulthood as "worried, underachieving, self-deprecating, and sometimes angry young men and women." Two out of three of the female children will show such "sleeper effects" as fears of failure and betrayal in their relationships with men. In other words, they are at great risk for failed marriages. Their use of alcohol and other drugs will be substantially higher than that of children from intact families.

Only three out of ten of the children will be described

as doing well. Nearly four of the ten will be clearly depressed, not be able to concentrate in school, have trouble making friends, and suffer from a wide range of other behavioral problems. Social scientists' conclusion: "Most of them will be on a downward course." Many of these children will become "overburdened," and frequently, firstborn children will wind up assuming far more responsibility than children their age can possibly cope with.

The divorce will be the hardest on kids between the ages of seven and thirteen. Some researchers think this is so because young school-age children are old enough to understand the concept of divorce, but not old enough to understand and deal with the emotional issues involved. Furthermore, when the conflict between parents continues after parental separation, it's almost inevitable that children will become embroiled, if not as pawns, then possibly as mediators. Either of these roles puts the children at great emotional risk.

As these children get older, we discover college students from divorced homes are more sexually active than their classmates from intact homes. And males whose parents were divorced before they were two years old are more sexually aggressive than other men. Males with divorced parents will hold the most permissive views relative to so-called recreational sex, and women with divorced parents will be more sexually active and aggressive than men or women from intact homes.

Oh, did I mention that these are the children of the parents in your group who are emotionally healthy, well-adjusted people from mainstream America? Also, these children are the ones who are doing well in school at the time of the divorce. Other children are in for a much tougher time, since the children I just described were from situations where the divorce was described as "divorce under the best of circumstances." The conclusion is clear that "divorce under the best of circumstances is terribly, tragically destructive."

THE OTHER SIDE—KIDS FROM INTACT FAMILIES

The Friday, January 19, 1990, issue of *USA Today* published a list of the twenty students on the first All USA College Academic Team along with forty who made the second and third teams. These young men and women were picked by a panel of judges, all educators, for their outstanding blend of scholarship, initiative, creativity, and leadership and for their willingness to use that talent to benefit others.

As I looked at these outstanding young men and women, one fact literally jumped off the pages. Namely, that eighteen of the twenty had their mothers and fathers listed, indicating they had come from a two-parent family. One of the young ladies had her husband listed (she could have come from a two-parent family), and one of the young men had only his mother listed (she could have been a widow). In other words, at least eighteen and possibly all twenty of these outstanding students had the enormous advantage of coming from a two-parent family.

This is *not* to imply that kids with only one parent can't make it. My wife and I were both raised by widows, and literally thousands of kids with only one parent have done extremely well. However, the evidence is solid that children from two-parent families have some measurable advantages.

PROBLEM CONSCIOUS OR SOLUTION ORIENTED?

If I were going to tell you how to go about having the best chance of preventing coming down with the flu, I would say things like, "Get plenty of rest because fatigue results in the body's inability to ward off germs. Eating properly will also give your body strength in the fight against these germs. Washing your hands frequently and keeping them away from your mouth and eyes will prevent transferring germs to your body, and regularly changing your toothbrush (as soon as you feel any symptoms, as you begin to feel

---

Are you problem conscious or solution oriented?

---

better, and when you feel you are over any sickness) will help you fight off colds and flu." My question is: Are you focusing on not getting the flu or staying healthy? The difference is subtle but vitally important.

Now, please don't misunderstand. I'm certainly NOT equating getting the flu with getting a divorce. I AM saying that our attitude about divorce—whether we are problem conscious or solution oriented—will make a major difference in our ability to regain the love we knew for our spouse (or gain it if it was never there).

For the rest of this chapter, I want to share some of the "germs" that lead to divorce and some ideas you can use in fighting the good fight.

WHAT CAUSES DIVORCE?_____

In 1976, almost one million marriages were dissolved, which is more than double the 1966 total of divorces. And the total number of divorces in 1988 was near the two million mark.

Obviously there are many reasons (or excuses) for these divorces. Recently I glanced at a copy of the *Minister's Marriage Manual*, compiled by Samuel Ward Hutton and used by many ministers around the country. As my eye scanned the various topics, premarital counseling, wedding etiquette, scriptural marriage ceremony, table of marriage laws, I was drawn to the heading "Grounds for Divorce." Those ranged from serious issues such as adultery or attempt on the life of the spouse, extreme cruelty or desertion to the commonly used "incompatibility." The only thing I didn't find in this list of grounds for divorce was the proverbial "coffee grounds"!

As we look at some of the reasons people divorce, it is with the hope that doing so will help prevent this tragedy from occurring in your life or the lives of others. And let me remind you that I'm not trying to make those of you who've been through the trauma of divorce feel worse than you already do. In these days of mail-order divorces, group divorces, and how-to books of "doing your own divorce," we have to look at the reality of this tragedy.

THREE "A's"

I have divided the reasons for divorce into *The Three "A's" of Divorce*. If you understand that our attitude toward divorce is so liberal—according to *U.S. News & World Report* the number one additudinal factor is the "no fault divorce"— and divorces are so easy to come by that they have become commonplace, *then* you get a picture of our problem. All reasons may not be contained in the three "A's," but if we follow the steps outlined, I believe we can eliminate over 90 percent of divorce in our country today!

Adultery—the Major Culprit

Leading the list of reasons for divorce as well as the list of grounds for divorce is *adultery*. Psychotherapist Les Carter, who conducts marriage seminars across America, has concluded that approximately 40 percent of all married men will at some time in their marriage have an extramarital affair. For those whose income is $70,000 a year or above, those chances rise to 70 percent. Furthermore, Dr. Carter points out that approximately 33 percent of married women will become involved in an extramarital affair, with the most vulnerable years ranging from thirty-five to thirty-nine. He points to four major reasons for extramarital affairs. Surprisingly, the first is unresolved anger. The second, excessive personal neediness. The third, craving for unbridled freedom. The fourth, a preoccupation with sex.

But perhaps you're thinking, what about those "innocent" parties married to the philandering spouse? Respected clergyman Dr. Stephen Olford suggests that perhaps they're not so innocent after all. He and many others have observed, as did Dr. Carter, that unresolved anger and other marriage conflicts helped contribute to the moral breakdown that may have caused the marriage disintegration, or as Dr. Olford says, "As a pastor in three churches encompassing twenty-eight years, I'm beginning to wonder if there really is such a thing as an innocent party." Certainly, in most cases, both husbands and wives share *some* of the blame and could have done more to hold the marriage together.

My point is this: For each of the four stated reasons for extramarital affairs (unresolved anger, excessive personal neediness, craving for unbridled freedom, and a preoccupation with sex), there are two steps to PREVENTION.

Step number one is RECOGNITION or AWARENESS. Watch for evidence or "symptoms" of a problem. How can you recognize an "affair" headed your way? Danger signals include the following: spending more time with your coworkers than with your spouse; sharing "secrets" with friends and coworkers; taking long lunches with the same person of the opposite sex; becoming defensive when questioned about your attitude toward a new "friend"; indulging in fantasy thinking about members of the opposite sex; having a "wandering" eye (taking special notice of handsome or beautiful others on a too-frequent basis); or exhibiting a complete disregard for this list.

The second step in preventive medicine is COUNSEL-ING. Each of the four reasons REQUIRES professional help. An objective, qualified person (NOT a caring friend) can help you deal with these areas in a positive manner. MONEY IS NOT AN ISSUE; IT IS AN EXCUSE. Today, many counselors have a "sliding scale" for payment based on income level, and many churches offer free counseling and "work-pay" programs that allow you to pay your own way. Think about this: You found a way to get that car, sofa, bedroom suite, washer/dryer, etc., when you couldn't afford it, so now you must understand that you CANNOT AFFORD NOT to get counseling.

Absence

The second "A" that leads to divorce is *absence*, which encompasses many marriage failures. The "busyness" of modern society is a primary culprit. We live in a go-go-go world that too often includes a dad who has turned into a workaholic as he pours his life into his career and a mom who has worked herself to exhaustion as she attempts to build a career and a marriage and handle motherhood at the same time. Over a period of time, both get so wrapped up in what they're doing that they drift apart and are absent from each other regularly. A feeling of isolation and indifference sets in. Gradually they stop listening and eventually they emotionally disengage. Many then acquire a "what's the use" attitude, and absence, which generally precedes separation, becomes a reality.

Adding to the reasoning or justification for absence is what Christine Wicker identifies as "the me-first family." In a series on the new American family in the *Dallas Morning News*, Wicker states that at least 80 percent of Americans are now living, to some degree, by a new code of behavior.

Individuality and self-fulfillment are valued more than ever. She bases her conclusion on surveys taken by Daniel Yankelvich and other social researchers over the past three decades. Such attitudes as "I'll stay married to you as long as it doesn't interfere with my career," "Our marriage is interfering with my personal fulfillment," and "We'd have children but we couldn't afford to maintain our life-style if we did" are reflections of this me-first philosophy.

Contributing greatly to this feeling, according to psychologists, social scientists, and investigative reporters, is the two-career family. As Paula England, an associate professor of sociology at the University of Texas at Dallas, says, "Women are kind of exhausted. They're also in a double bind." She points out, "The ones who work feel they've abandoned their children to day care; the ones who stay home feel they are abandoning their own career and prospects."

Finding Fault as if There Was a Reward for It

Many times when husbands and wives become disenchanted with each other, they start looking for things to be unhappy with and to gripe about as far as a mate's "faults" are concerned. Over a period of time, they talk themselves into the idea that all the problems of life would "go away" if they just got rid of that "no-good I'm married to." In other words, ABSENCE becomes the permanent solution instead of the problem. Three visits at a "Parents Without Partners" meeting (if children are involved) would persuade them that divorce might solve *some* problems, but it would present a whole new set of "challenges" that are, in *most* cases, worse than the ones they currently have.

Franklin C. Bailey, counselor for the conciliation court of Los Angeles, lists several other factors identified by the ten thousand individuals who have passed through his office. He says sex, money, children, and trouble with in-laws lead to serious marital problems. Yet Bailey, who runs what he calls "the busiest repair shop in town" that is "just around the corner from the busiest wrecking business"—the divorce court—notes the real problems are *selfishness* and *greed*. And I say these can be overcome by spending time, quality *and* quantity time, together and fighting off the terrible "A" of absence.

Take the two steps necessary to save your marriage: RECOGNITION of the problem and COUNSELING by a professional. To recognize that absence does *not* make the heart grow fonder, take notice when: you spend more time at work than at home or more time pursuing recreational activities than being with family; you see your spouse talking but aren't hearing the words being said; you recognize that you are just "going through the motions" with no zest for living in family activities; your body is at home and your mind is anywhere else.

Counseling can help you focus on the problem (obsessive-compulsive behavior, preoccupation with "minor priorities," or poor listening skills) rather than the *symptom* of the problem. This focus will lead toward a solution.

Abuse—a Solvable Problem

The ugliest "A" of them all is *abuse*, whether it's chemical or physical (which are often linked). Statistics for 1988 from the National Coalition Against Domestic Violence reveal that three to four million women are beaten each year in their homes by husbands, ex-husbands, or lovers. Psychologist Constance Doren notes that approximately 60 percent of the abusers with whom she has worked were themselves abused or saw their fathers abusing their mothers. Abuse is a definite factor in many divorces, and yet in most cases it is a solvable problem.

Dr. Robert Geffner, an associate professor of psychology at the University of Texas at Tyler and one of the country's leading experts on the subject, reports that domestic violence affects somewhere between 20 and 30 percent of American women. According to Dr. Geffner, the problem usually develops in a very gradual process. He explains that it usually begins with verbal intimidation, then graduates to physical abuse.

Geffner and others explain that, contrary to popular belief, most men who batter don't turn out to be monsters (authorities speculate only 10 percent are psychopathic). With the majority of these men, battering is a *learned* behavior. They were battered as children, or they witnessed it in their own family, so they see abuse as the norm. Since *any* behavior that has been learned can be *unlearned*, I strongly encourage the abuser to get into counseling even before you finish this book. If you have *any* love for your mate (in most cases your wife), yourself, or your children, you will take steps immediately to bring an end to this destructive behavior.

Now, it's not my purpose here to spend a great deal of time on this unpleasant subject except to note that a Minneapolis study published in *U.S. News & World Report* documents that when family members *are arrested, repeat offenses occur only half as often as when the suspects are not charged.* The point is crystal clear: When the abuser *knows* he is going to be held accountable for his conduct, he manages to exercise considerably more control over that conduct.

In the case of chemical abuse, treatment is the *only* answer. The disease of alcoholism or other drug abuse requires a level of professionalism only offered in certified treatment centers. Waiting is foolish. Treatment is the *only* answer, because God is at the foundation of all treatment programs that work. Alcoholics Anonymous, Narcotics Anonymous, and all "12-step programs" identify God as the key to recovery.

The Doctor Remembered

A number of years ago, I read about a wife who was periodically subjected to severe beatings by her physician husband when he occasionally came home in a drunken stupor. The abuse happened about twice each year, and after each episode, the husband would be very remorseful, apologize profusely, say he had no idea of what he was doing, ask for her forgiveness, shed buckets of tears, and promise to never, never hurt his wife again.

For years this faithful, loving wife forgave and continued to live in fear. Then one morning about eleven her husband awoke from his drunken stupor to see her quietly seated in a chair across from the couch where he had passed out. As the cobwebs started to clear, she handed him a cup of coffee. He drank the coffee, then started with his usual apologies, explanations, pleadings, and tears. She quietly listened, and after about twenty minutes, she calmly said, "I accept your apologies and understand that you really do love me and that you really didn't know what you were doing. I believe you when you say that you will never hit me again. However, let me tell you what I have been doing this morning. I just got back from a professional photographer's studio. He has taken pictures of every part of my body that has a bruise. I have the negatives that are in safekeeping. I've made arrangements so that if anything happens to me, those negatives and the detailed statement of what has been happening all these years will be turned over to the police.

"After I finished that assignment, I went by the office and made a copy of the list of your patients. Just to make sure you don't forget your promise to never beat me again, let me share with you what I will do if you 'forget.' First, I'll send copies of the pictures I just had made to all our friends and social contacts as well as the medical society. Next, I'll send the pictures and a cover letter to all your patients."

Interestingly enough, over twenty years later the good doctor had never "forgotten" that beating his wife was a "no-no," and with counseling their marriage had changed over the years from a tension-filled nightmare to a loving, caring relationship. Obviously there were additional pieces to that complex puzzle, but my point is twofold. First, I repeat, any time a responsible person is held accountable for his conduct, that conduct is more likely to be responsible. Second, we can change, and in this case, both the abused and the abuser were much, much better off.

I tell the story of the doctor and his wife to make another major point as well. An abusive home is a miserable place to live, but counseling and some creative approaches to solving the problem could be infinitely better than divorce. Remember that about 90 percent of the men who abuse their wives are not "monsters" and can be helped—if you follow our two-step approach: RECOGNITION and COUNSELING.

To recognize the "warning signs" of abuse, you must be sensitive to: releasing an uncontrolled temper; "striking out" with words *before* thinking; slamming doors, books, cabinets, papers, etc.; having an urge to hit something when confused or angry. Counseling can help us deal with all areas of abuse, including emotional, sexual, and economic abuse.

THE REASON FOR DIVORCE

The overriding questions are: How many divorces really *should* take place? How many times do *all* parties *benefit* because of the divorce? Are there any legitimate *reasons* for a divorce?

The answer to the last question is "yes." The Bible clearly states that adultery is definitely grounds for divorce, and with AIDS as a factor in our lives, sexual promiscuity is

now a matter of life and death. I'm also convinced that the
Bible says a wife has a right and a responsibility to separate
from a husband who is psychopathic and is physically abusive of her and/or the children. She must do what needs to
be done to protect her children from a father who sexually
abuses them. Many times separation, if not divorce, is the
only viable option.

Having made these comments, let me state that I believe
in most cases with prayer, common sense, hard work, and
counseling the marriage can be saved and can be restored to
a good, solid, even romantic relationship.

GUILT-FREE DIVORCE

If, after all this, you still think divorce may be for you,
let me share with you a way in which I sincerely believe that
you can have not only a "positive divorce" but one that can
prevent a lifetime of guilt and regret.

If you will follow the five steps I am recommending—
with number five being divorce—I am convinced you can
have the best of all worlds.

1. Hold a "summit meeting." Set aside a minimum of
twenty-four hours away from your home and all distractions. Unplug the phone and the television. Take all meals in
a cafeteria or restaurant. Spend the first hour writing down
any and all grievances against your spouse (you will have
more time later if you need it).

At the end of sixty minutes, even if you're not through
writing—or have been through for fifty-nine minutes—swap
papers. There is to be no talking during this time.

After you have reviewed the writing, follow the guidelines for fighting fairly on page 201 (holding hands, facing
each other, having chairs twenty-one inches apart, etc.).
Spend as much time as necessary for discussion. For every
hour in discussion, take a fifteen-minute break. Nothing

more intimate than holding hands is allowed during this summit meeting. You must "stay at it" for a minimum of eight hours.

2. *Attend a marriage encounter weekend or "Born to Win."* You and your spouse can attend a marriage encounter weekend seminar or our three-day workshop in Dallas, "Born To Win," where you can receive objective input that will give you direction in your life and marriage.*

3. *Read.* Read every book and pamphlet you possibly can that is written by an author basing his or her principles on God's Book. Much outstanding material is available to help you with your specific situation—regardless of how unique and strange it may seem to you. For the sake of following the steps to guilt-free divorce, a minimum of three books of at least 150 pages each is required. (See the Appendix for ideas.)

4. *Seek Counseling.* Seek a counselor for each of you individually and another counselor for both of you together. Again, investigate the background and training of these individuals. Many states don't have formal certification programs for all counselors. Some counselors are "self-proclaimed" experts with master's or doctorate degrees in vaguely related fields. Be careful! Two organizations that are credible Christian counseling concerns are New Life Clinics (1-800-NEW-LIFE) and Rapha (1-800-227-2657). Call the 800 numbers for more information or for a counselor near you, or investigate through your church.

A minimum of six months' counseling is required to continue working toward a guilt-free divorce.

5. *Divorce.* If you have thoroughly completed all four of the previous steps, you may consider divorce . . . but my

---

*Episcopal Marriage Encounter, 1-800-851-3779; A Weekend to Remember, Family Ministry, 501-223-8663; Worldwide Marriage Encounter, 714-881-3456. "Born To Win" Seminars, contact Zig Ziglar Corporation, 3330 Earhart, Suite 204, Carrollton, TX 75006, 1-800-527-0306.

belief is that you won't! You see, if you take all these steps, divorce will VERY RARELY be a viable outcome (except for the reasons mentioned on page 67).

And now, the best news of all. All that energy you have been using in finding fault with your mate or in thinking about divorce can be spent in concentrating on how you can "court" your spouse more effectively. With that kind of focus, THE BEST IS YET TO COME!

P.S. An anonymous author contributed this thought: Every husband and wife should remember that you go into marriage with your eyes wide open, but you'll stay in the marriage only if you keep them half shut. Obviously this addresses the fact that you keep them half shut to your mate's faults and "peculiarities." You obviously leave them wide open to your mate's good qualities and all acts of kindness and affection.

4 O.K., I'M CONVINCED—LET'S START OVER

A man and woman should choose each other for
life for the simple reason that a long life is barely
enough time for a man and woman to understand
each other and to understand is to love.
—Dr. George Truett

If we are going to start the courtship process over, the first
thing we need to do is determine to *fix the cause* and not
place the blame. For too long, too many people, including
husbands and wives, have pointed the finger of blame at
others and said it's "his" fault or "her" fault. Placing the
blame is not exactly a new concept since this practice actually began in the Garden of Eden. You remember the story:
God had put Adam and Eve there, in the lap of luxury, and
He gave them free run of the most beautiful piece of prop-
erty on the face of the earth. Their only instruction was not
to eat the fruit of a specific tree in the center of the Garden.
Whether you read the Bible or not, you know what happened. Adam and Eve were disobedient. They ate the fruit.
That evening, as God was walking in the Garden, He called
out (this will not be verbatim), "Adam, where are you?"

ADAM: Over here, Lord.
GOD: Adam, did you eat that fruit?
ADAM: Lord, let me tell You about that woman You gave
me!
GOD: Eve, did you eat that fruit?
EVE: Lord, let me tell You about that snake!

And, of course, the snake didn't have a leg to stand on!

Now, for my theologically knowledgeable friends, I recognize that I'm on shaky ground when I say the snake "didn't have a leg to stand on." But I am on sound theological *and* psychological grounds when I say that *you* don't have a leg to stand on when you start blaming everything and everybody for the difficulties in your marriage. Obviously others can have a negative impact; but the truth is that you are where you are with your mate because of a series of choices you and your mate have made. When you accept the responsibility for making the proper choices, you receive the opportunity to make your marriage better *and* more exciting.

THE SIMPLE TRUTH

At this point you might be thinking, "Come on, Zig. Everybody knows you start at the beginning!" But think with me for a moment. See if the following "rings a bell" for you.

"When we began dating, things were wonderful. I couldn't live without her—" "He was the apple of my eye. Since that time, he's become like a speck in the eye." "—I can't live with her."

My point is, regardless of how good or bad the marriage has been, we sometimes have to "*re*start" at the very beginning. In fact, Dr. George W. Crane, the psychologist who wrote the psychology textbooks I studied when I was in college, says that if you have fallen out of love with your mate, go back and court like you did when you first fell in love, and you will fall back in love. Think about it. If your marriage is in trouble, or if you want to make it even better, you've got nothing to lose by "starting over."

A friend of mine says that we live at a time in history where we have become a task-oriented society. Children learn to tie their shoes—task completed. Students study for tests, take the exam—task completed. Young adults interview for the job, get the job—task completed. Adults set the goal to become director, supervisor, vice president, or owner, and when they "arrive,"—task completed. Married couples plan to relocate, make the move—task completed. Older adults make out wills—task completed. Throughout most of our lives, we are checking off completed tasks on our "to do" lists. Courtship cannot be checked off as completed—it is an ongoing process, not a task.

FOR BETTER *AND* WORSE

To paraphrase psychologist Bob Wubbolding: Can you think of anything at this moment you could do to make your marriage worse? The odds are rather high that you answered "yes" to that one. With that in mind, the next question becomes obvious, doesn't it? Is there anything you can do that would make your marriage better? And the answer to that one is equally obvious, so the major purpose of this book is to explore the ways that will allow you to make your marriage better.

Can you think of anything at this moment you could do to make your marriage worse?

In the same breath, I hasten to add that just as health is more than the absence of illness, a happy marriage is far more than the absence of conflict. A happy and exciting relationship with your mate can—and should—get better and better as the years go by. A sound marriage does not mean the absence of any conflict; it does mean handling the conflict in a proper manner. In *Courtship After Marriage*, you will learn some exciting concepts as to how you can communicate and avoid conflict (well, most of it). You are even going to learn to "fight" so that both of you emerge as clear-cut winners.

Speaking of conflict, those of you reading this book who were born after 1960 and those who believe strongly in the feminist movement may struggle with the next few paragraphs. Let me encourage you to be open-minded and have the courage to "hang in there" even if you disagree because I have something special to say to you that you *may not* have heard before now!

LET'S TURN BACK THE CLOCK

You surely remember how you felt when you first met your husband and how you, with enormous excitement, told your mother that you had met *HIM*. Obviously, you did not have to explain to Mom who *HIM* was. The light in your eyes said it all. And you fellows remember that first date—how enormously excited you were, and though you lived only a couple of miles from her, you left an hour early just in case you had that flat and, lo and behold, that's exactly what happened. Not having a spare, you had to walk a mile to a service station where you got your tire repaired and headed back to your car. In the process, you were running late and had gotten a little greasy, so you quickly called your beloved and explained you would be arriving a little late, but you would be there. She responded that she understood, no problem, and she would be ready when you arrived.

Obviously, she was not ready when you arrived. She made you wait the few minutes that any self-respecting girl will make a first-time date wait. When she did make her entrance, it was a grand one. She had on that big smile, putting her best foot forward, showing her most photogenic side, and grinning like she had just walked through a swinging door on somebody else's push. You, obviously, were elated to see her. As the two of you left the house, despite the fact she had been running up and down those front steps for the last eighteen years, you were concerned that she would be unable to negotiate them on her own, since they were nearly *six inches* high, so you "helped" her down the stairs.

You were then confronted with a monstrous car door that no female should ever be expected to open, so you opened it for her and helped her in, closing the door gently and firmly to make certain she was safe and secure. You then drove to the movie, and in the lobby, you loaded up on popcorn, candy, soft drinks, and all the goodies. You devoured yours as quickly as possible, sat quietly for a few moments, and then you made your move. According to the planning you had carefully done a week in advance, you suddenly felt the urge to stretch. As you stretched, it just happened that when you let your arm come down, it landed right on her shoulder. Surprise, surprise! You clever rascal!

After the film, the two of you left the theater chatting excitedly about the movie, so absolutely preoccupied and fascinated with each other. You stopped off at the neighborhood hot spot, sat back in a corner booth drinking Cokes—splitting a piece of pie—noise, music, and conversation all about you, but you had eyes only for each other. In fact, you were able to sit there talking about anything and everything. Fellas, you're talking *and* listening because whatever she says is utterly fascinating. Gals, you think he is the sharpest, wittiest, neatest individual you've ever met. Remember how it was? Remember how *good* it was? Remember how much *fun* you had? AND THEN ONE DAY YOU GOT MARRIED.

ROMANCE SHOULD START, NOT END, WITH MARRIAGE

So what's the problem? It's the scientific law called the second law of thermodynamics. This law states that any closed system, left to itself, tends toward breakdown. That principle includes marriages. Relationships tend to disintegrate, unless we put time and energy into sustaining them.

Strange, isn't it, how you initially planned everything to the "T," how you connived to get your girlfriend off by herself, how you figured out every way possible to hold her hand, put your arm around her, what you were going to say, and how you were going to say it. AND THEN ONE DAY YOU GOT MARRIED. Most marriages do not end in a blowout. They gradually die because of a lot of slow leaks that take away the joy, excitement, and enthusiasm that man and wife really can enjoy. A major reason for this loss is that we become so accustomed to having each other around, assuming we have now learned everything about each other, we make little or no serious effort to cement the relationship we worked so hard to bring about, and we start taking a lot of things for granted.

THE MARRIAGE ATTITUDE

I'm really talking about an attitude. Starting over to build a successful, loving marriage depends on having the right "marriage attitude." You must understand that marriage is not a fence to hem you in; it's a guardrail to protect what's inside. Several years ago, The Redhead and I were driving through the beautiful Colorado mountains. From time to time, we would see a sign that said "mountain overlook." On many occasions we stopped, and there was a guardrail that enabled us to walk right up to the edge and look at the magnificent scenery. We felt much more secure having that guardrail and were able to enjoy the spectacular view because of it.

That's really the way marriage should be. The security of knowing that you have someone to love, to trust, to encourage, to laugh with, grow with, and enjoy life with and that he or she is yours—and yours alone—makes marriage so incredible! Marriage is not designed to place restrictions on you; marriage is for the purpose of completing you, thus enabling each member of the "team" to be more than you could be as individuals. Marriage is designed to enable you to grow to your maximum because of the support, love, and encouragement of your mate.

We see the "expanding-to-the-maximum" concept demonstrated on school grounds. In the inner-city schools, if there are no fences, the kids congregate and play primarily toward the center of the yard. If there is a fence, however, they play right up to the very edge of the street and, I might add, in safety. A good marriage affords the excitement of utilizing all our abilities and yet provides the safety of protecting the one we love.

"A wife wants a husband who listens, is understanding, is confident in himself, has security in his job, is dependable, is an achiever, is aggressive but with humility and is trying to make the marriage better."
—Dr. Richard Furman

In marriage, your spouse is looking for a mate who will accept responsibility rather than pass the buck or the blame. My good friend Dr. Richard Furman, in his book *The Intimate Husband*, points out, "A wife wants a husband who listens, is understanding, is confident in himself, has security in his job, is dependable, is an achiever, is aggressive but with humility and is trying to make the marriage better."

For fear you zoomed past those last seven words, let me repeat them, ". . . is trying to make the marriage better." Any marriage, almost regardless of how good it is, will ultimately go bad unless both husband and wife make a conscious decision to work on making the marriage even better—and then take the steps to do exactly that. At that same time, any marriage, regardless of how bad it is, has an excellent chance of not only surviving, but flourishing, if both husband and wife take the positive approach *and* start taking the steps necessary to make the relationship work.

Survey after survey indicates that the number one source of satisfaction in our lives is a good marriage, rating above fame, fortune, good jobs, or even good health. Over and over, happily married couples and marriage professionals acknowledge that a good marriage is viewed by most not as a means to some other end but as an end in itself. That's the kind of marriage attitude that will make "starting over" for you a happy and loving success. Now let's dig deeper and carefully explore "starting over" in depth.

STEP ONE: RESPECT YOUR MATE _____

This respect factor certainly stood out in a story that hit all the newspapers concerning Nolan Ryan, the tremendous pitcher for the Texas Rangers. The year 1989 was incredibly successful for Nolan. He had been signed as a free agent by the Texas Rangers from the Houston Astros, and at age forty-two, he had recorded well over two hundred strikeouts and had an excellent won-lost record. Everyone just knew that since he was pitching with a one-year contract with an option for another year, he would automatically sign for that one-year contract extension, especially since he had made baseball history by recording his five thousandth career strikeout during the course of the season. I might add that he would also make more than $1 million for the coming season. However, before Nolan Ryan agreed to accept the Rangers' offer for the next year, he had a long discussion with his wife concerning all the pros and cons. The bottom line is, her input was the determining factor in Nolan's decision.

There's a tremendous lesson for every husband who reads these words. In the procedure that Nolan Ryan followed, he showed his wife the ultimate respect by the length and depth of their discussion and the fact that he valued her input so much. You can bet they are friends and their relationship is a special one.

Later in 1989, many people were encouraging Nolan to run for political office as Texas Commissioner of Agriculture. They felt he had an excellent chance to be elected because of his public profile, his extraordinary public acceptance, and his unique qualifications for the job. However, Ryan again took the same approach. He consulted with his wife, and together the decision was made that the timing was inappropriate. Any CEO worth his salt will certainly consult his executive vice president on decisions concerning their relationship and their happiness. He will also keep her informed, as I stress in another chapter, by talking with her about the "little things" that happen on a daily basis.

STEP TWO: MAKE FRIENDS WITH YOUR MATE

One of the most important components to make yours a super, harmonious, working-together marriage is to become each other's best friend. Psychologists point out that in the happiest and strongest marriages, the spouses play not only the roles of lovers and partners, but best friends as well. In fact, as a marriage progresses over time, the friendship will deepen, and the marriage partners may become even more like each other. In a study of 125 couples, researchers found that many of the spouses became more similar in intelligence, perception, and motor skills as the years went by. In addition, all of us have noticed that some couples, over a period of time, literally begin to look like each other.

In his book *The Friendship Factor,* Dr. Alan McGinnis points to a current shortage of friendships in our country, citing our mobile society as one of the biggest hindrances to developing long-term friendships. This trend, in my opinion, certainly underscores the importance of husband and wife being best friends.

Deep and lasting friendships take time—lots of time. That time invested with your mate brings many rewards. You can truly form a deep and lasting friendship and become "best friends." In my opinion the two most negative words ever put together are the words *quality time.* The words contradict each other and have wrecked many marriages and caused emotional damage to many children.

According to Dr. Nick Stinnett, the statement "The amount of time you spend with your spouse is less important than the quality" is just a marriage myth. In a recent survey cited by Dr. Stinnett, more than 90 percent of the couples who considered their marriage "strong and close" also said they spent a great deal of time together. The survey also observed that divorced couples usually had spent little time together before the split, so as you "start over," I encourage you to take time AND . . .

STEP THREE: BUILD A FEW SAND CASTLES_____

Many divorces could be prevented and more fun could be had if husbands and wives took time to plan more activities with each other and with the entire family. And friendships within the entire family would grow.

For example, in the summer of '89 we experienced a rare, magnificent vacation in Myrtle Beach, South Carolina. Our entire family, including our three daughters and their husbands, our son and his wife, and the grandchildren, was there. The circumstances were truly marvelous. We were able to find a large home to rent, so each family had a private room and bath. It was a fun-filled, carefree vacation, and we had a chance to see some beautiful sights. All of us enjoyed taking a dip in the ocean, and the golfers in the family got in a fair amount of time on the golf course. However, it was the unanimous opinion of everyone there that the sand castle experience was the highlight of the entire trip.

Our son-in-love, Jim Norman, took the initiative and decided he was going to build a sand castle. He invited all of us to participate. Naturally, in the initial stages the younger ones were the most enthusiastic. Jim is quite a craftsman, so he proceeded to design and dig a marvelous structure. The sand castle (and it truly was a "castle") was about six feet long, four and a half feet wide, and about three feet tall; it was complete with a moat, drawbridges, gates, towers, stairways, storage rooms, sleeping quarters—the whole bit. As you might imagine, the unique project took several hours to finish.

As the day wore on, lots of people stopped by to see what was happening, and that evening, as the tide started to come in, the onlookers increased in numbers. Some of them stopped for a couple of minutes and made small talk before they moved on. Many of the beach walkers, as well as every member of the family, gathered as the tide rose toward the castle. The first wave that crossed the moat and got into the ditch was greeted with a round of applause. Later, when the waves were large enough to reach the moat and completely encircle the castle, there was a loud cheer followed by a spontaneous burst of applause. And guess who was leading the applause? That's right—ol' Zig himself! In addition to the family, at that moment there were about forty other people from many states; yet a spirit of friendship and brotherhood was born right there on the beach.

The next day was even more spectacular. Jim had gotten so carried away with the spectator success of the day before that he set up and designed—this time on paper—a far more elaborate construction. He started the day by going to the hardware store and buying a "serious" shovel so that he could dig deeper and faster and with less effort. He started at 8:00 A.M., and if the structure the day before had been outstanding, this one was truly incredible. It was about twice as big in size, and the designs and everything else were even more elaborate. He created new ways of developing battle stations, stairways, storage units, living quarters, moats, drawbridges, and all the specifics of a *real* castle.

Needless to say, we took a large number of pictures of the construction. Jim got so involved that he literally forgot about eating and worked right through the lunch hour. Again the crowds gathered in larger and larger numbers. A camaraderie was established with lots of people; and children, grandchildren, husbands, and wives all felt a unique closeness with one another. (After all, it was *our* project.)

Again, when the tide started coming in, we had the same experience we'd had the evening before—the applause, the cheers, the whole bit. It was truly delightful.

Now if you think for a moment, my daughter and her husband had come in from California; the rest of us had driven from the Dallas-Fort Worth area. There we were, anywhere from thirteen to twenty-five hundred miles away from home, spending significant parts of two days hovering around a sand castle and having a marvelous time in the process. It's safe to say that not only did my children and grandchildren enjoy themselves, but I'm convinced that in each instance, my children and their mates grew a little closer because of this shared event. They had another incident in their memory book to help them cement their marriages, make friends with their mates, and start thinking about and planning for their own extended families.

The point I'm making is simply that families of long-term duration who are friends and have love and concern for one another can have a grand time doing simple things. Needless to say, you don't have to go to Myrtle Beach or anywhere else to have this kind of experience. The process of taking the time to be together is a marvelous way to build a solid foundation for real friendship and a long-term courtship process.

STEP FOUR: MAKE THE COMMITMENT

The importance *and* the effectiveness of commitment were best demonstrated in the answer we received from the survey we conducted on couples who have been married twenty-five years or more *and* who would marry the same person again. We believed quite strongly that most of these couples would feel that marriage was a lifetime commitment, but we were pleasantly surprised to discover that 100 percent of the couples felt that when they said "I do," they literally meant for better and for worse as well as for life.

The dictionary says that *to commit* is "to entrust, to pledge, to obligate, to find." According to Dr. James Olthuis, marriage partners who do not consider their relationship a permanent trust for life will find themselves living in permanent crisis, unable to tolerate each other, quarreling, sulking, and having difficulty with even the mildest criticism. In an eloquent analogy, Dr. Richard Dobbins pointed out that "adhesive tape is not made for repetitive use." He went on to say that the strongest bond adhesive tape is capable of making is formed with the first surface to which it is applied. You can remove the tape and reapply it to other surfaces, and it will still adhere. However, with every application, some of the adhesiveness has been lost. His point, and the facts support his position: The *first* marriage can and should "adhere" or bind two people closer and stronger together than any other relationship they can form.

A classic example of commitment is the one given to Myrtle Georgia Dillingham by James Dobson, Sr., her husband-to-be, a few months before the wedding. The statement, along with some comments by Dr. James Dobson, Jr., their only child, says a lot. Among other things, the statement and comments help us to understand why the marriage was such a good one despite the differences in the makeup of the two people:

> I want you to understand and be fully aware of my feelings concerning the marriage covenant which we are about to enter. I have been taught at my mother's knee, and in harmony with the Word of God, that the marriage vows are inviolable, and by entering into them I am binding myself absolutely and for life. The idea of estrangement from you through divorce for any reason at all (although God allows one—infidelity) will never at any time be permitted to enter into my thinking. I'm not naive in this. On the contrary, I'm fully aware of the possibility, unlikely as it now appears, that mutual incompatibility or other unforeseen circumstances could result in extreme mental suffering. If such becomes the case, I am resolved for my part to accept it as a consequence of the commitment I am now making, and to bear it if necessary, to the end of our lives together.
>
> I have loved you dearly as a sweetheart and will continue to love you as my wife. But over and above that, I love you with a Christian love that demands that I never react in any way toward you that would jeopardize our prospects of

entering heaven, which is the supreme objective of both our lives. And I pray that God Himself will make our affection for one another perfect and eternal.*

How could a young man only twenty-three years of age make such a mature pledge? How could he make a lifetime commitment with so much certainty? Obviously, his words would amount to an empty promise if he were relying on his own wisdom and hopes. (A 50 percent divorce rate today proves the fallibility of man's best intentions.) The answer lies in the fact that he was basing his marriage relationship on the principles authored by God Himself. Those precepts had been tested and found true for thousands of years. The marriage of James and Myrtle lasted forty-three years—until death temporarily came between them. They never veered from the wedding vows exchanged in 1934, and they enjoyed all the blessings God intended for a permanent relationship between a man and woman.

Of course, this does not mean they spent every moment in perfect bliss. James and Myrtle were as different as night and day, and they struggled mightily to harmonize their diverse temperaments. While he was contemplative and introspective, she was active and outgoing. Where he was intellectual and reserved, she was practical and profoundly social. "James, Sr. enjoyed being with other people, but if given his preference, he would rather be alone painting, reading, or studying," a family member said. "Myrtle, on the other hand, loved fellowship. She never wanted to miss a single conversation. She wanted to be in on everything."

Their son also observed these characteristics. "They both had intense personalities and saw everything differently, even though they were absolutely committed to each

---

*Rolf Zettersten, *Dr. Dobson: Turning Hearts toward Home* (Waco, Tex.: Word, 1989).

other," he said. "When it came to the important, overriding decisions, my mother always yielded to the leadership of my father. She had profound respect for him. Nevertheless, they could argue endlessly about such mundane things as how to pack suitcases into the trunk of a car, or which hotel to select for the night. But if an idea ever got past both of them, you knew it was good."

Here's Commitment

Will you turn and face each other. Join your hands together. Jim, repeat after me. I, Jim, take you, Joyce, to be my wedded wife. To have and to hold, from this day forward, for better, for worse, for richer, for poorer, in sickness and in health, to love and to cherish, till death us do part, according to God's holy ordinance and thereto I pledge you my love.

Joyce, repeat after me. I, Joyce, take you, Jim, to be my wedded husband. To have and to hold, from this day forward, for better, for worse, for richer, for poorer, in sickness and in health, to love and to cherish, till death us do part, according to God's holy ordinance and thereto I pledge you my love.

With a sparkle in their eyes and joy in their hearts, Jim Cowles and Joyce Cobb repeated the vows shown here. Today they are more in love than ever. I'm convinced (or their example would not be in this book) that their marriage not only will survive and be a happy one, but will be more loving and meaningful as the years go by.

What a beautiful event the wedding was! The most unique aspect (and Joyce confided in me that it was one of the most meaningful to her and Jim) was the commitment this couple made to their "new" set of parents. Here is what happened:

PASTOR: *I'm going to ask Jim and Joyce, if they would, to kneel here before us; I'm going to ask both sets of parents, if they would, to come forward.*

I'm going to ask you parents if you will join hands with one another because when a couple gets married, it's not just the couple uniting—in addition, there's going to be a bond between the parents. In the days of Jesus, one of the reasons a couple would get married would be to strengthen the family. Now this family's going to be strengthened because of this ceremony today.

And now, the bride and groom would like to speak to each of you.

JOYCE: *Mom Beth and Dad Sid, I want to thank you two so much for raising Jim in a home where Jesus was welcome, and for instilling in him the qualities and character I so needed in a husband. I promise you that I'll be to Jim the wife that you would hand pick for him. I love you two.*

JIM: *Howell and Jean, I thank you very much for this beautiful, Godly woman that you've raised; and I also thank you for Jesus being welcome in your home; and I know that He's the leader of your home; and I promise to you to try to love Joyce as Jesus really does love the church. I promise to be faithful and true, and I hope to be the best that she could ever have.*

Now *that* is commitment!

Commitment Means Forever!

Commitment, incidentally, includes a decision in advance to seek reconciliation in the event there is difficulty in the marriage. Even as I write these words, I think of a close friend of mine who died suddenly in 1985 at age thirty-nine. My friend and his wife had a most unusual marriage. Both of them were fine, fine people, but their marriage was surely one of the stormiest I have ever known about. They had made a definite commitment early on to make their marriage work, but for whatever reason, it seemed to be impossible. They would live together but then separate.

If my life depended on it, I could not tell you if the problem was his fault or her fault, but as my mother would say, there are always three sides to every story: His side, her side, and the right side. This I do know—they had trouble. This I also know—they desperately wanted their marriage to work. They sought counseling. They did everything humanly possible to make it work.

Shortly after my friend's death, his wife told me that they had "gotten it all together" in the months immediately prior to his death. In glowing terms she described to me the joy, excitement, and even ecstasy they had experienced during that time frame. She said to me that those last few months made all of the years of effort worthwhile—that they had experienced a happiness for months that many people never enjoy even for a day. She also told me she believed that their children would remember their mother and father all their lives for the relationship they had during those months. Without stating it point-blank, she was saying how grateful she was that she and her husband had kept trying to make the marriage work. By doing everything possible to "grow" their relationship into something special, they achieved a success and happiness that many people never achieve because too many husbands and wives give up too soon.

I once heard a counselor say, "You can't scrub the deck of a sinking ship." He was making the point that some marriages are too far gone to save. In some cases, serious and irreparable damage has been done, but let me encourage you to get off the deck and get into the engine room. Locate the source of the excess water your ship is taking on and do everything possible to stem the flood. If you will look for reasons to stay married, instead of reasons to part, you will find them. Where do you start looking? Well, I'm glad you asked!

STEP FIVE: REBUILD THE FOUNDATION

I'm convinced that if the basic commitment and the character foundation are there to build upon, as in the case of my two friends who had the courage to "keep on keeping on," every marriage can be an enduring one. Most can be a pleasant experience, and many can be truly beautiful, romantic, and exciting. I emphasize the character foundation, though, because as the Blackfoot Indians say, "You can't carve rotten wood."

Renewing the Covenant

On November 29, 1983, I participated in a most unusual ceremony in Lubbock, Texas. My long-term friends, James and Juanell Teague, were celebrating their twenty-fifth wedding anniversary, and they wanted to exchange their vows again. They asked me to "officially" perform the "unofficial" ceremony. Because it was unofficial (I'm not licensed to perform weddings) and because of our friendship, I agreed. In the process of planning and preparing for the occasion, the concept of a covenant occurred to me. A *covenant* according to the dictionary is a "solemn agreement; compact, the Promises of God as recorded in the Bible." Because marriage is so sacred and the restating of those vows so important, I took my assignment very seriously. Here is the covenant:

Covenant
ONE LOVE SHARED BY TWO

Because we, _____ and _____ have chosen to become "one," we quite naturally want our marriage to be successful, happy, and permanent.

To accomplish this objective, we individually and jointly pledge to respect, encourage, and support each other as individuals. We further agree to insure the success, happiness, and permanence of our marriage by keeping the promises stated in our marriage vows and in this sacred covenant.

Understanding that marriage is under attack and the family is in trouble, we promise to demonstrate to the world that a truly committed husband and wife, with God's help, can have a beautiful marriage and grow in love for one another in the process.

Accepting the fact that God is the Author of success in marriage, and believing the best way to stay in His will is to stay in His Word, we agree to seek His will and direction every day by reading the Bible and humbling ourselves before Him in prayer.

Because God specifically promises, "For them that honor me I will honor," we solemnly promise to honor God in every phase of our individual lives as well as in our life together.

Knowing that the fellowship of believers gives encouragement to individuals and support to the family structure, we agree to make a maximim effort to attend worship services together each week.

Believing that marriage is ordained and blessed by God, we pledge our love and faithfulness to Him and to each other. Being aware of the frailties of man and recognizing the probability of falling short of this lofty objective, we further pledge to love, honor, and forgive one another even as God, for Christ's sake, has loved, honored, and forgiven us.

We thank God for bringing us together and ask Him in His Providence to keep His hand on our marriage, and to heal any hurts we inflict upon one another. Because we now more completely commit this marriage to Jesus Christ, our faith assures us that under His watchcare, "The best is yet to be." We reverently enter this sacred covenant because we know these pledges and procedures will completely assure greater happiness and permanence of our "one love shared by two."*

---

*If you and your mate would like a copy of this covenant on parchment, suitable

STEP SIX: BECOME PARTNERS FOR *LIFE* _____

The story about Sir Edmund Hillary and his historic climb of Mount Everest gives us a classic example about a partnership and friendship attitude that will build a great marriage. While becoming the first man in history to reach that mountain peak, Sir Edmund was accompanied by his trusted native guide, Tenzing Norgay. After scaling the mountain, Sir Edmund lost his footing on the way down, but Tenzing held the line taut and kept them both from falling to their deaths by digging his axe into the ice.

When questioned later, Tenzing refused any special credit for saving Sir Edmund's life. He considered it a routine

---

Mountain climbers (and committed husbands and wives) always help each other.

---

part of the job and expressed his feelings simply, but eloquently, when he said, "Mountain climbers always help each other."

What a fantastic philosophy for marriage partners to adopt! They should always help each other. After all, it really is true that you can have everything in life you want if you will just help enough other people get what they want. When you get close enough and stay close enough to help your mate, you really will be making that fresh start. Based on observation and personal experience, I can tell you that "starting over" can be fun and exciting.

---

for framing, send us an 8½ " x 11 " self-addressed envelope with three first-class stamps, and we'll be happy to send you one. The Zig Ziglar Corporation, 3330 Earhart, Suite 204, Carrollton, Texas 75006. P.S. As you read this covenant together, I encourage you to initial each one of the eight parts before you sign the covenant.

5 | IT'S COURTING TIME

You can do it gradually—day by day and play by play—if you *want* to do it, if you *will* to do it, if you *work* to do it over a sufficiently long period of time.
—William E. Hall

Little things make big differences. For example, fellows, there's a dramatic difference in results when you refer to your one and only as a "vision" instead of a "sight." There's just a day's difference in time, but there are light years of difference in results between telling your beloved that she looks like the first day of spring and telling her that she looks like the last day of a long, hard winter.

The little things really do make the big difference.

On the serious side, seventeen years ago I went on a diet and exercise program. I lost 37 pounds in ten months by losing 1.9 ounces per day. I wrote *See You At The Top*, a 384-page 2,000,000-copy best-seller, by writing an average of 1.26 pages every day for ten months. People who are successful at whatever they do reach their objectives by a series of little things they do every day. If you will do the little things I am suggesting (on a daily basis), they will make a big difference in your relationship with your mate.

"Action often precedes the feeling."
—Zig Ziglar

As I share this series of action steps husbands and wives can do to help romance last a lifetime, I'd like to stress that some of these "little" things will make a dramatic difference almost immediately while others will take time. A lot depends on the condition of the marriage at the moment and whether you take the steps grudgingly because you've got "nothing to lose" or whether you take them with a loving, expectant attitude. But please hear this:

Regardless of your attitude when you start the procedures, the physical process of doing them will ultimately produce results because *feelings* follow actions.

HERE'S A GOOD PLACE TO START

When our son, Tom, was in the fifth grade, he brought this little formula home from school. Follow the recipe, which is guaranteed to "cook up" a happy marriage. Take one cup of love, two cups of loyalty, three cups of forgive-

---

"Logic won't change an emotion but action will."
—Zig Ziglar

---

ness, four quarts of faith, and one barrel of laughter. Take love and loyalty and mix it thoroughly with faith; blend it with tenderness, kindness, and understanding. Add friendship and hope. Sprinkle abundantly with laughter. Bake it with sunshine. Wrap it regularly with lots of hugs. Serve generous helpings daily, and you've got a marvelous recipe for that happy marriage.

Following one simple guideline will really keep your marriage cooking and help make your mate your best friend. The guideline, "The Golden Rule," clearly says that you should do unto your mate as you want your mate to do unto you. Please notice that the instructions say that you are to go first or initiate the action. Following are some action steps you can initiate!

"SPOIL" EACH OTHER

There really are many instances when husbands and wives need to "spoil" each other. You can bake him a cake or prepare a special dish you know he enjoys. Whether you and the kids enjoy the dish or not is unimportant; you prepare that dish just because you love him. If you send him off to work with a cold lunch, be sure to include a warm note in that lunch to warm it up a bit. Just let him know that you'll be looking forward to seeing him when he gets home in the evening. Not a big deal, but it can make a great deal of difference.

Spoil your spouse.

A little thing like calling your mate during a coffee break is no big deal, but over a period of time, little things do make a big difference. A hole in the ground is nothing at all, and yet you can break your leg if you step into it while walking fast or running. A simple little thing, like regularly opening the car door for your wife, can make a big difference in the long run.

In the forty-three years we've been married, I honestly don't believe my wife has opened her own car door a dozen times when we've been together. Now, obviously, she's physically capable of opening that door, but I personally feel good when I'm privileged to do such a simple little thing like opening that door for her. It serves as a constant reminder to me that she is important, and I want to be constantly aware of taking the action steps that say, "I love you."

One reason mothers love their babies so much is that they have to do everything for them when they are babies. I am personally convinced that if a husband gets out of the car and leaves his wife sitting there without opening the door, she should sit on the horn and embarrass him for not acting like the gentleman he really is and treating her like the lady she is. In a restaurant, when the wife gets up to go to the rest room, the husband should, out of respect, stand and hold her chair for her. It says to her—and to others— "This is a special lady. She's the one I love. She's important to me. And I delight in doing little things for her," announcing to everyone in sight, "This is my lady." Gentlemen, I can tell you with absolute certainty, that little process will delight your wife.

I COULD DO IT MYSELF

You could easily argue that those little things are time-consuming, that the wife is certainly capable of doing those things, and of course, you would be 100 percent right. But, by the same token, there is no reason why I could not get my own cup of coffee in the morning, pour my own cereal, and get my own fruit. There is no reason at all why I could not even pop my own popcorn, but, ladies, I can tell you that when The Redhead does one of those things, we both enjoy it. She is saying simply, "Honey, I enjoy doing this for you, so you have a seat and let me do it."

When I come in from an engagement and I arrive home at nine or ten o'clock in the evening, what an absolute delight to smell popcorn when I walk in the front door! Now, I could have bought the popcorn at the airport, or I could take five minutes and pop it myself. However, my wife delights in doing that, and it says to me, "Honey, I want to give you a special welcome home; I've been thinking about you, and I've been missing you."

Now, don't get "hung up" on the actions themselves. Instead, try to understand the principle. I have a friend who despises yard work. He says that he never met a lawn mower he couldn't hate! To his credit (and good fortune), he married a woman who loves yard work (especially mowing the grass). This arrangement is very "foreign" to me because I was raised with the belief that yard work was man's work— and I still think it is! But these happily married people are taking advantage of their personal likes and dislikes to please each other. My point is this: Doing those "little" things (whatever they may be) will definitely enhance any marriage and keep romance alive and well. I'm personally convinced it's simply little, thoughtful things that have enabled my wife and me to stay in love. As a matter of fact, we're more in love today than we were when we first married, or even after we had been married twenty years. That's true, not because we do those little things, but because we are willing, even anxious to do those things.

Little acts of thoughtfulness can score lots of points with your mate if they show love and concern. For example, in our home, when my wife uses the frying pan or roaster (they're both heavy and, quite frankly, difficult to clean), I, as a general rule, will at least take over that part of the cleanup process. Since I spent fourteen years in the cookware business, I know all the techniques of cleaning them until they shine to a standstill. The Redhead always breathes a sigh of relief and expresses her heartfelt thanks.

On her side, The Redhead considers my travel schedule and always checks to see if I need any dry cleaning done. No big deal—unless I have a special need for a certain garment. If I haven't had the time or the opportunity to go to the cleaners, then it's a "big deal." Her time investment is only a few minutes, but those few minutes make a big difference to me.

VOLUNTEER

At any time you see your mate struggling with a difficult day or a heavy work load, you should take the initiative and simply say, "Honey, you're tired. Let me do this for you. Why don't you sit down, and I'll put the children to bed tonight." Or "I'll pick up all the clothes and items that have been left around." Or "Let me brew the coffee, do the grocery shopping, vacuum the den, etc." Many things can be done to ease your mate's path and make your own life and marriage happier.

If husband and wife are both working outside the home, dealing with the children, preparing the evening meal, and doing the laundry do not fit under the category of "women's work." These tasks are family responsibilities and, I might add, opportunities. If the family includes a husband and a wife and a couple of children, that means four people created the work. Since four people help to create disorder in the home and make a lot of work necessary, if only one is doing the work, an impossible burden is placed on that one. You function as a team. It's that simple.

THANK YOU, HONEY

When your mate does *anything* that you appreciate and that makes your trip through life a little easier, a sincere "thank you" is important and appreciated. The reality is that if you "expect" your mate to do something because it's his or her "job" or responsibility, the odds are long that the job will be done reluctantly, poorly, or not at all. If you "appreciate" your mate for doing it, results are far better. Makes sense!

Here's a chance to say, "Thank you, Honey," for

- wearing my favorite dress to the reception.
- taking the cat to the vet.
- picking up the kids from Mom's.
- baking those sweet potatoes.
- calling our bridge partners for Saturday night.
- fixing lunch for us. I was exhausted.
- taking the lawn mower to the shop.
- swapping your day off so we could extend our weekend.
- preparing the low cholesterol lunch.
- building such a nice fire.
- giving up your football game so I could watch the Ice Capades.
- bringing all those groceries in from the car. They were so heavy.

Those "little" thank-you's are indications of *class*. My mother told me many times that we might not all be rich and smart but we can all be kind and courteous. And for what

---

Nothing is so strong as gentleness; nothing so gentle as real strength

---

it's worth, as I've dealt with leaders in business, industry, and government, I've noted that almost without exception in hundreds of cases the higher up in the organization, the more courteous and polite these men and women are. De Sales was right: "Nothing is so strong as gentleness; nothing so gentle as real strength."

I'M SORRY, HONEY

Many times husbands and wives act considerably less than mature (would you believe "childishly" and "selfishly"?)

when they hit a snag in their relationship, and stubborn pride (hardheaded arrogance might be more accurate) erects a serious roadblock in the marriage. For example,

HUSBAND: If she showed more affection, I'd come home earlier and wouldn't stop by the bar.

WIFE: If he came home earlier, I'd show more affection.

Remember, when disagreements take place, *who* makes the move to "make up" isn't important; however, the one who makes the move demonstrates the greater maturity and love, as well as the greater concern that the marriage not only will survive, but thrive in an atmosphere of love and understanding. And when *you* are wrong, the most important words in your vocabulary are, "I'm sorry, Honey; I made a mistake. Will you forgive me?"

THIS IS MY MATE

Incidentally, the way you introduce your mate says a great deal about your relationship. One of my real delights is to be able to say to people, "This is The Redhead. This is the one you hear me talk about all the time. I love her, and I am very proud to be able to introduce her to you as my wife. This is Jean."

In our three-day "Born To Win" seminar in Dallas, we lead the married couples through a series of exercises that culminate in the husband and the wife introducing each other to three different couples. Each person uses a "new" introduction just written that points out at least one likable thing about the other. For me, I love to point out The Redhead's beautiful smile or intuitive, sensitive nature. From my side, there is so much to choose from, it's hard to pick just one thing.

The bottom line is that when husbands and wives are truly proud of their mates, the relationship is enhanced considerably. It's also true that the more times you indicate that deep pride in your mate, the more things you will discover in your mate to be proud of and the better the relationship will become.

TIME OUT

My good friends, Phil and Carol Glasgow, started something really neat back in 1981 when their children were ages two, two, and five (not twins, they adopted one while Carol was pregnant). With three preschool children, Carol obviously was one more busy household executive. Fortunately, Phil was very sensitive to his responsibilities and Carol's needs. In one of their quiet discussions, the idea was born that it would be good for the kids, good for Carol, and good for Phil if, on occasion, they made a rather drastic change.

The idea was that Carol would take off once a year for five or six days (and three or four times for a day or two). She would go to a beautiful resort or hotel. She would sleep as late as she wanted to, have room service, spend time in the sauna, in the beauty shop, or around the pool, etc. In the meantime, Phil and the kids would be back home doing their thing. Phil would be spending all of his time playing mama *and* daddy.

They have done this once each year, and they both agree it is one of the best things they have ever done. Carol returns home rested and relaxed and hungry for those little arms (the big ones, too) to be around her neck.

An exhausted Phil, with a brand-new appreciation for the role his wife plays, is elated to see Carol and to take off on a vacation of his own—back to his regular job.

A less elaborate and more affordable approach may be comparable to what one friend of mine received from his wife on their anniversary. When he arrived home from the office, very tired from a hard day, she said, "Honey, we need to run one errand before dinner this evening." Giving him directions by a circuitous route, she took him to one of the nicest luxury hotels in Dallas, where she had arranged a special weekend of relaxation together. Similar options may include fixing your spouse his favorite food or taking her to that absolutely incredible restaurant she's always wanted to visit.

I recognize that none of these approaches (especially Phil and Carol's) would fit the budget of many families, but, husbands, here's an affordable challenge. On a regular basis, especially if there are small children involved, give your wife complete freedom for the day. Get up early with the kids, prepare their breakfast, and take care of their *every* need. Your wife could visit friends, shop a little, have lunch out, catch a movie, walk in the park, and "live it up" in general.

In the meantime, dad is back home looking after the kids and gaining a new appreciation for his wife and the mother of his children. This approach enables both husband and wife to gain a new respect and admiration for each other. The kids win, too, because they get to know their dad much better when he spends time with them doing the things that mom normally does.

Don't be alarmed, and please don't you husbands and wives misunderstand. You don't need to break the bank, and for that matter, you don't need to spend any money at all. A quick note in the mail or a long, carefully thought-out love letter will do wonders for your spouse. A sincere note or card will deepen the love felt for you, boost the self-image, and give the marriage the encouragement that all marriages really do need.

With careful budgeting and planning, most couples can "squirrel" away, on a regular basis, money for a heavy date or short weekend trip where you can devote 100 percent of your time and attention to each other. The time for each other is the important issue, not where you spend that time.

You can set aside, on a regular basis, time for a casual walk, just so you can be in a "together" situation. An unhurried stroll will open the door of thoughtful conversation, and you'll be amazed at how much a thirty- to sixty-minute walk will do for the marriage, especially if it's done on a regular basis. From time to time, you need to turn off the TV and devote your time and attention to each other. This assures your mate that he or she is important to you, especially if you look each other in the eye as you talk.

YOUR MATE WILL LOVE THIS

On those occasions when it's possible and she's out doing some shopping or going somewhere with the kids, if you beat her home and prepare the dinner, you will score a tremendous number of points, and your time investment will be very helpful to her. And, ladies, when he does things like that, even if the meal doesn't turn out to be the equivalent of what a good French chef would do, I encourage you to express your gratitude for the effort and find something good to say about the results. Just remember, husbands and wives, that as I said earlier, your mate doesn't live by bread alone; he or she needs to be "buttered up" from time to time.

> **Your mate doesn't live by bread alone; he or she needs to be "buttered up" from time to time.**

For example, I'm convinced that if the ladies handled everything as well as they handle the cooking on the outdoor grill, our marriages would be much better off. I do not ever remember hearing a lady say she was better on the outdoor grill than her husband. In every case, they go into great detail about what a magnificent cook he is on the grill, how he just has the touch with a steak or fish or chicken or chops or whatever he decides to cook. For that reason the husbands of America are almost unanimous in their dedication to proving that their wives are absolutely right, that they really do have the master's touch when they get to the outdoor grill. Don't misunderstand. I wouldn't accuse you ladies of being manipulative under any circumstances, but I do find it interesting that that particular technique has worked wonders for keeping the husbands active in cooking outside. I'm just wondering if it wouldn't work as well on the inside? You've certainly got nothing to lose, ladies. After all, these men do love to hear the praise of the one they love!

Now! A short commercial for sex. (The long one comes in chapter 7.) While these "little" things apparently have nothing to do with the sexual relationship between husbands and wives, they actually have everything to do with that relationship. The joining together of a man and his wife in the ultimate intimacy of the sexual act is the most beautiful and meaningful aspect of the relationship, and all aspects of the relationship are improved by gentle acts of kindness, consideration, and thoughtfulness.

WELCOME HOME, HONEY

For many years I have done considerable amounts of traveling to meet my heavy speaking schedule. Most of my seminars take place in the late afternoon or evening with a typical one finishing at, or shortly after, 10:00 P.M. Generally speaking, I'm pretty tired because the energy drain for a three- to four-hour seminar is considerable. However, for a number of years, I've always headed for home if I could make it by 2:00 A.M. Here's why: I'm always lovingly and enthusiastically welcomed home. Whether The Redhead has been asleep four minutes or four hours, she *always* gives me a big hug and tells me how glad she is that I'm home.

That's not normal. Every husband and wife who will ever read these words has got to know that *nobody* feels good *all* the time. Nobody wakes up from a deep sleep and is always pleasant and caring. Nobody, that is, except The Redhead. That's the reason I'm willing, even anxious, to miss a little sleep to spend the rest of the night with her and to wake up in my own bed the next morning.

But that's not all. If either of us returns home, even from a grocery trip, and the other one is there, a greeting, a hug, and a quick kiss are always exchanged. As I often say, she is affectionately known as "The Happy Hugger," so that shouldn't be too surprising. But here's my question: Doesn't it make sense that if you and your mate made it a point to greet each other as pleasantly and affectionately (well almost) as you did when you were seriously courting each other the first time, the spark in your romance would at least maintain a steady glow?

A SENSE OF HUMOR IS IMPORTANT

In our hurry, hurry, rush, rush, do it now, instant everything world with all the distractions we face in life, in our family, and specifically in our marriage, surely one of the most effective tools at our disposal to keep romance alive and a relationship open, loving, and caring is a sense of humor. In this department I hit the jackpot with The Redhead. She has one of the best senses of humor I've ever encountered. Interestingly enough, she seldom, if ever, tells a joke. Too many people think only comedians enjoy humor in life. The Redhead sees humor in many situations in life and expresses herself with a hearty laugh that delights me and others who hear her.

I never cease to be amazed at the conversations she has

on the telephone; though I can hear only one end, I'm always amused and entertained with the amount of laughter injected into the conversations. This is true almost regardless of whom she is talking with. She can have a thirty-minute conversation with any one of her children, but especially her daughters, and two hours later hold another thirty-minute conversation, and both conversations will be punctuated with a considerable amount of laughter. I've often said that I'd rather listen to one side of her telephone conversation than watch anything I've seen on television.

On my side of the ledger, I, too, have a sense of humor and see humor in many of life's daily situations. I've studied the impact of humor on individuals and audiences and turn to humor in my personal, family, and business lives regularly, hopefully in a natural and effective manner. I tell jokes, do a little "leg pulling," and share one-liners in my everyday life. Despite the fact that The Redhead seldom does any of these things, the reality is that she has a better sense of humor and enjoys humor even more than I do. So, regardless of your ability to tell or remember jokes, you can still enjoy the marriage benefits of a good sense of humor.

LIVE TOGETHER AND LAUGH TOGETHER _____

I encourage you as husbands and wives to do things together that will enable you to laugh. Interestingly enough, all of the people I've ever encountered will tell you that they enjoy humor, that they like to laugh, that truly funny things are enjoyable to see. Yet very few of them spend any time developing and utilizing their own sense of humor. There are a number of joke books available that are funny and clean; and there are some truly humorous movies that we all can benefit from. *Reader's Digest* and *Guideposts* magazines are excellent sources of humorous and inspirational materials. Our own Zig Ziglar Corporation *Top Performance* magazine contains some humorous, enlightening, and inspiring articles. Your local library is an excellent source of humorous materials.

There are some enormous benefits from laughing. In his book, *Anatomy of an Illness*, Norman Cousins points out that a real good "belly laugh" is "internal jogging." He turned to laughter as part of his cure for cancer after doctors had given him odds of less than one out of one hundred to survive. He rented movies and videos of his favorite comedians and entertainers and watched them daily. The laughter had a substantial impact on his attitude, offered him hope and encouragement, and gave his internal organs a real workout. Norman Cousins used laughter to help overcome the odds and survive!

When I speak of humor and laughter, I'm obviously talking about good, clean humor that never is of the "sick" or put-down variety. I'm not talking about ethnic or racial jokes; I'm talking about situational comedies that take place all around us every day.

DEVELOPING A SENSE OF HUMOR _____

My friend, Dr. Issac The Clown, gives us some marvelous reasons for developing a sense of humor:

> Laughter is one of the greatest mental tonics known to man. It is the second most powerful human emotion we as people can express (the first being love). Laughter can dispel anxiety, help manage stress, depression, fear and worry. It can stimulate the healing process. Laughter provides strong medical, psychological, social and even spiritual benefits. Laughter is like internal jogging. It enhances the respiratory system, helps oxygenate the body, relax tense muscles, and is an all

around pain killer. It will lower pulse and blood pressure. Laughter can pave the way for a new and exciting outlook on life. It is the universal communicator that can cross all boundaries of race or culture.

You can't laugh and be mad; you can't laugh and worry. Stress, worry and laughter are not compatible.

Laughter is low calorie, caffeine free, no salt, no preservations or additives, 100% natural, and one size fits all. Laughter is truly God's gift. You can get high on laughter but never OD.

Laughter is contagious. Once it starts, little can be done to stop it. Laughter never felt bad, committed a crime, started a war or broke up a relationship. Laughter is shared by the giver and the receiver. Laughter costs nothing, and it's non-taxable.

Laughter is a trend setter. If we can find ways to laugh first thing in the morning, it may, in fact, set the trend for the rest of the day. One of the most constructive uses of laughter is when we can laugh at ourselves. If we can laugh at ourselves, we leave little room for others to laugh at us.

Humor can be found in just about every daily situation. We just need to stop and think, and just take a good look around us and we can always find reasons to share joy.

Laughter is saying, "I'm O.K. You're O.K." It's a way we can accept what we can't change.

The clown inside of us need not be the one with a bright colored costume and painted face. It may just be a reflection of something that was lost sometime ago. The personal clown inside of you may be the one who felt that life was a joy and well worth living. He or she may be the one inside of you that needs other people, and that can live in harmony with others. Laughter can be the driving force to make life alive again.

Incidentally, I'd like to repeat myself and stress that you do not need to tell jokes or "entertain" to develop and enjoy a sense of humor. However, the effect humor will have on every area of your life will be substantial. I've never known a person with a real sense of humor (the Bob Hope, Red Skelton, Carol Burnett kind, not the Rodney Dangerfield, Joan Rivers, Milton Berle kind) who did not have lots of friends. To paraphrase an old cliche, husbands and wives who laugh together will love together and *stay* together.

Now, combine that sense of humor with some old-fashioned optimism, and you have two powerful components that will go a long way in a marriage.

THE WIDOWED WOMAN

A gentleman moved into a home for the retired and on the first day found himself seated directly across the table from a widow. After a few minutes he became uncomfortably aware of the fact that she was staring at him. He tried to avoid her gaze but to no avail; those stares kept coming. Finally, after several minutes of this, he asked her why she was staring so intently at him. She responded, "I'm absolutely amazed!"

MAN: Amazed at what?

WIDOW: The incredible resemblance you have to my third husband! Your color, your size, your height, your weight, your mannerisms, *everything* reminds me so completely of my third husband!

MAN: Your third husband! How many times have you been married?

WIDOW: Twice.

I COME BEARING GIFTS

Somebody once said we all like to be understood and we all like to feel important. All of us like to be remembered on our birthdays, anniversaries, Valentine's Day, Christmas, and other special holidays. I am at this moment looking at a birthday card The Redhead gave me about ten years ago. The front shows two little animal comic strip characters, and the card reads, "To my husband," and these two characters say, "Kiss-kiss, hug-hug, clutch-clutch." Then on the inside, the comic strip character with a heart above the head says underneath it, "It never hurts to review the basics. Happy Birthday, with love." And The Redhead simply wrote, "From your own Sugar Baby." The word *own* is the one that moved me. *Your own* spoke volumes saying, "I am yours," and it carried the unspoken though strongly implied message that "you are mine."

We should also remember those occasions when there are no occasions. Drop your mate a note in the mail, "just because." Pick up a single flower and take it home, "just because." Call from time to time during the day and tell your mate you love him or her. When you have occasions to choose gifts, choose them with care, thinking in terms of what your mate would really want.

If you are the recipient of a gift you are less than enthusiastic about, let me remind you that behind the gift is a thought and the person who had that thought is your mate. Your mate chose the gift because he or she wanted to please you. So, husbands, if she gave you after-shave for your birthday, use it after you shave. Don't leave it on the shelf 'til next year so you can pitch it out during spring cleaning. If she gave you a sweater, and you don't particularly enjoy wearing sweaters, go ahead and wear it on occasion anyway. Your using the after-shave or wearing the sweater is a gracious way of saying, "Thank you for loving me and thinking of me when you bought this gift." Wives, if he chooses the wrong color or fragrance, just remember that he was thinking about you and only you when he made the purchase. You can truly love him and thank him for that.

When your mate makes a mistake and buys a gift you

don't want, please don't do what I saw one lady do. She publicly berated her husband for buying her a dress that was
the wrong size and color. She told him in no uncertain terms
that he should know she wore a smaller size and that green
was not her color. What she effectively did was discourage
him from ever again attempting to buy her anything of a
personal nature or perhaps anything at all.

I KNOW I'M BRAGGING

I know this sounds like I'm bragging, but because it's
true I'm going to tell you. In the forty-three years we've been
married, I've never made a mistake in choosing a gift for The
Redhead. It's always been something she wanted very badly,
and something she absolutely loves. If it's an article of clothing, it's always the right size, and even though my color coor-
dination skills are minimal, it's always the right color. I just
flat have never made a mistake in selecting gifts for her.

Now, I'll be the first to admit that sometimes I never see
the item again, because she's exchanged it for the right size
or the right color, or for something she did want. What she's
done is very simple: She's made me feel good and made it
awfully easy for me to try again. In short, she encouraged
me to do what I really love to do—tangibly express to her
how important she is to me.

Just one little tip, fellows. If you buy your wife an article of clothing and you're not certain about the size, make
the error in a smaller size and save the sales slip.

Please understand that whether the gift is a ten-carat
diamond, a cruise around the world, or a two-dollar item, it
isn't the gift itself but the thought behind the gift that really
counts. As Sir Lancelot said, "The gift without the giver is
bare." Another poet expressed it beautifully when he said,
"Rings and jewels are not gifts, but apologies for gifts. The

only true gift is a portion of oneself." In short, husbands and wives, don't get carried away with "things" you give your mate, but do give yourself—and from time to time, a simple gift or card or, even better, a handwritten love note or letter is a marvelous devotion to your mate. Its *cost* is zero; its value is enormous.

By now, you could be thinking that this courtship after marriage takes a lot of time. You are right, but the return on time investment is enormous. Not only are the ongoing rewards exciting, but it takes considerably less time to maintain a loving relationship than it does to repair a broken one.

6 THAT'S NOT WHAT I SAID

The right word spoken at the right time is as
beautiful as gold apples in a silver bowl.
—Proverbs 25:11 EB

The fiftieth anniversary is a very special occasion, and in the small midwestern community everyone wanted to honor this couple, so the city really rolled out the red carpet. The festivities included a breakfast celebration where the mayor spoke; one of the local service clubs sponsored a noon luncheon; friends of the family gave an afternoon tea reception; and an anniversary dinner with just the family participating concluded the activities. At about ten o'clock that evening as the big day was drawing to a close, the man and his wife were finally alone.

As was his custom, the husband went to the kitchen, prepared a piece of toast and a small glass of milk, and called his wife to announce that it was ready. She walked into the kitchen, took one look at the snack, and burst into tears. The husband was naturally puzzled and concerned, so he embraced her and asked what the problem was. She tearfully explained that she had thought that on this most special of all days he would have been more thoughtful and not given her the end piece of bread. The man was silent for a moment, and then he quietly said, "Why, Honey, that's my favorite piece of bread."

The irony is that for all those years he had been giving her what he considered to be the best and she had been accepting it with the feeling that it was the worst. The tragedy is that had they just been talking and listening while sharing their likes and dislikes, much pain could have been avoided. The natural question that follows is this: How many other "misunderstood moments" had occurred throughout the marriage because they did not share their feelings about a thousand and one different things?

Of course, that's a simple example, but an amazing number of husbands and wives really do not do a very good job of communicating.

SHARE THE DETAILS

Now, this will not come as a great shock to you, but men and women are different. Beyond the obvious differences, there are many subtleties. However, there is nothing subtle about the differences in the area of verbal communication.

Studies involving hidden microphones on little boys and girls prove quite conclusively that at an early age, not only do little girls talk more, but they are substantially more skilled and effective in their communications. They enunciate more clearly, and their words are more easily understood.

It has been estimated that in a typical twenty-four-hour day, the average woman voices some 25,000 words while the average man verbalizes 10,000 words. Unfortunately, the man invests about 9,000 of his words in his typical workday, and his wife invests about the same number in her workday. When they get back together in the evening, his verbal bank account is approaching bankruptcy while her verbal bank account contains a surplus that must be used by midnight or lost forever.

The woman often *needs* to talk and *needs* to hear her husband invest part of his verbal bank account by telling her on a daily basis of his love for her. As a matter of fact, somebody once asked when a man should tell his wife he loved her. The wit responded, "Before someone else does!" Yet another man confessed in bittersweet irony that he loved his wife so much that sometimes it was all he could do to keep from telling her. In yet another case, I heard of a man who hadn't told his wife he loved her in over twenty years and then shot the man who did!

Behind these slightly humorous/slightly truthful "slices of life," there is a serious message. Talk, listen, and communicate with your spouse. It is a fact that on average, women do talk more than men, and on average, they need to hear more from men.

Yes, I know averages are often misleading. For example, if you were to put one foot in a bucket of ice water and the other foot in a bucket of boiling water, on average, you would not be comfortable. I also know you can drown in a river that has an average depth of only seven inches. However, I can say with considerable confidence that in the communication department the average American woman is more interested in details and "small talk" than the average American man. (But who wants to be average?) Actually she has a real need, and a sensitive husband meets that need by investing a solid part of his verbal bank account in significant *and* insignificant small talk. *And* he listens with interest as his wife shares her feelings and invests her verbal bank account in him.

NO ONE IS IMMUNE

Probably the one area in which The Redhead and I have had the most difficulty throughout our marriage has been the area of communication. Most people would assume that since I earn my living primarily by speaking, writing, and doing video and audio training programs, I'm the bubbling, detail-oriented conversationalist at home. My wife will assure you that such is not the case.

I well remember a meeting with the executive staff at our company that lasted over four hours. We went into many of our plans for advertising, marketing, direct mail, and an overall approach to a new system of distribution. The meeting was lengthy and exciting. When I arrived home, The Redhead naturally asked the question, "How did it go?" I responded, "Really fine." She said, "What did you talk about?" And I replied, "Well, we got involved in some details of advertising and direct mail; we talked about a couple of new products, and some new ideas on marketing, and that was about it."

She looked at me with that "Now, come on, Zig, you can do better than that" grin and said, "Honey, you were in a meeting that lasted several hours. You have now spent less than sixty seconds telling me what took place." Normally, I talk a little more than that, but the point is the same. Women want more details than men do, and in this area all of us could improve if we really started thinking in terms of what will meet the other person's needs and make him or her happier in the process.

DIFFERENT INTERESTS AND PERCEPTIONS

An important facet of building a healthy marriage is understanding that not only are men and women "different," but they have different interests and perceptions. For example, about five years ago, my brother, Judge, and his wife, Sarah, were visiting in our home and for some reason a convention we had attended in Daytona Beach, Florida, in 1952 was mentioned. In order to put a handle on circumstances and the event itself, Sarah said to Jean, "You remember that convention, Jean. That's the one Sybil Small wore the blue dress with the white collar and belt. She had the little blue-and-white hat to go with it, as well as blue-and-white shoes." The Redhead acknowledged she remembered. I looked at my brother; he looked at me; we both broke out in laughter at the same time. I then said to Judge, "You remember that one, Boy! That's the one where Earl had on the brown suit, the brown-and-white tie, and brown-and-white shoes." And, of course, we laughed even louder.

Question: What man would remember what someone else had been wearing thirty-three years ago? My only point is this: Husbands and wives must clearly understand that there are vast differences—and that those differences don't make one any better or any worse than the other— differences simply mean each of us is unique. When husbands and wives learn to deal with those differences in a kind, loving, and gracious manner, our chances of having a romantic relationship all our lives will be greatly enhanced.

THEY'RE ONLY "WORDS"

Words were important to Thomas Carlyle, but he didn't realize just how important until after the death of his wife, whom he sometimes neglected in life. In his diary was found what has been termed by some the saddest sentence in the English language. Carlyle wrote, "Oh, that I had you yet for five minutes by my side, that I might tell you all."

C. S. Lewis in *Reflections on the Psalms* wrote,

> It is not out of compliment that lovers keep on telling one another how beautiful they are. The delight is incomplete 'til it is expressed. It is frustrating to have discovered a new author and not be able to tell anyone how good he is, to come suddenly at the turn of the road upon some mountain valley of unexpected grandeur and then have to keep silent because the people with you care for it no more than for a tin can in the ditch, to hear a good joke and find no one to share it with.

IF YOU CAN'T TALK, WRITE

A poet once said that those who do not show their love do not love. I'm not certain that's completely accurate, but I know there are many husbands and wives who are loved but have no assurance of that love. In those cases, the mate is so non-expressive that whether or not they are truly loved is pure guesswork. There are many people who will protest that they are "just not very good at expressing themselves," and that they show their love in other ways. While every act and evidence of love is important, a mate needs verbal reassurance (a note is pretty good, too) on a regular basis of being truly loved. (It literally takes only one second to say "I love you," and you can emphasize each word in three seconds.) In most cases, the man is not the expressive one and does not verbalize his feelings or demonstrate his affections unless he wants to express them through sexual involvement with his wife. This causes his wife to feel used, not loved.

For people who do not verbalize very well, I would like to remind you that you apparently verbalized well enough before you were married to persuade your mate to marry you. This indicates that your *ability* to communicate is not the problem. Your lack of interest or even unwillingness to communicate is the major problem.

The sad truth is, many times husbands and wives, even after years of marriage, still have difficulty discussing everyday involvements ranging from painting the front porch to deciding who takes out the kitty litter. One of the reasons for the breakdown is that many times the mate who opens the conversation has been interrupted before completing the thought or feeling. On occasion one mate finishes the sentence, word, or thought for the other one. Incidentally, the offending party might not be fully aware of this annoying habit. This thoughtless habit definitely is irritating and too many times closes the lines of communication. Oftentimes the one who opened the conversation feels a "what's the use" attitude and then stubbornly refuses to make any further effort to continue the conversation.

If you recognize any signs of communication problems in your home, let me urge you to write a letter to your mate and either mail it or place it in a spot where your mate will be sure to find it when you're not around. This gives you the advantage of being able to carefully—and less emotionally—state how you feel without fear of either interruption or rejection. Written communication also demonstrates a willingness, even an eagerness, on your part to solve the problem and open those lines of communication.

I encourage you not to bring out a laundry list of perceived ills or problems, but to lovingly and factually state your desire to draw closer to your mate by being able to express your thoughts and feelings. Be careful not to attack your mate personally. Instead, address your concerns, your feelings, and the problem as you perceive it. Use phrases like:

- "I always feel bad when we hit a roadblock in our communication efforts."
- "It's amazing how each of us communicates so well with others, and yet we seem to have difficulty communicating with each other."
- "Would you help me to understand why this happens and what I can do to help us find a solution?"
- "I'm not blaming you. I'm just saying there is a problem, and we certainly want to solve it so we can get on with loving each other."
- "I feel bad when I am unable to express my concern in an acceptable manner, especially about some things that mean so much to both of us."

Trying to just say the words I have written here will come across as "patronizing" and won't solve the problem, so put these statements in your own words and share them with complete sincerity. If you will carefully choose *your* words prior to the "moment of emotion," you will be much better prepared to handle the situation.

IF YOU'RE WRONG, APOLOGIZE _____

Be courageous and apologize when you make a mistake! For example, "I know I should have called you last night to let you know I was running late, but a phone really was not handy and driving out of the way to find one would have delayed my arrival even more. Next time I will do better so that you will at least know that I am alive and well and headed in that direction. Why don't we sit down tonight and just talk about this communication problem?" You might write a short note saying, "I apologize for not picking up the bath mat this morning, and I understand that upsets you. I'll try to do better next time. P.S. Thank you for the delicious meal last night. You really outdid yourself on that one!" Only insert that last line if the facts are obviously true. Insincere flattery will not help your case at this point.

You can disagree without being disagreeable.

Actually, in many cases, when you acknowledge that you have made a mistake, you are encouraging and laying the groundwork for a more open and loving relationship with each other. A gentle, loving attitude is the key. People who are "*brutally* frank" and "let it *all* hang out" are courting disaster in any relationship. Honesty *and* compassion are important companions. All of us disagree from time to time, and it's a sign of maturity when we can disagree without being disagreeable.

For what it's worth, when you are wrong and admit that you made a mistake and ask forgiveness, you clearly establish the fact that you're wiser today than you were yesterday. I don't believe your mate would hold that one against you! Remember the Biblical admonition found in Ephesians

---

"Be ye kind one to another, tenderhearted, forgiving one another." —Ephesians 4:32 KJV

4:32: "Be ye kind one to another, tenderhearted, forgiving one another" (KJV). We need to also remember that until we forgive each other, God is not going to forgive us (Matthew 6:14–15). Kindness and gentle communication are often the keys that unlock the door of forgiveness.

ARE YOU LISTENING?

There's another crucial ingredient in communication. In fact, in some ways an even more important ingredient than saying the right thing is *listening!* Many marriage counselors say that not listening is the number one problem in families today. Studies show that poor listeners have less satisfying marriages as well as less successful careers. (You *can't* respond to a message if you didn't "get" the message.)

The results of a widely publicized survey stated that 98 percent of the women surveyed wished for more "verbal closeness" with their male partners, and the most frequently cited cause of women's anger was "He doesn't listen." Seventy-one percent of the women surveyed said they had given up and no longer even tried to draw their husbands out. That's sad *and* a sure sign of a "sick marriage." Fortunately the illness need not be fatal, and it won't be if you practice the communication techniques we're covering.

HERE'S HOW

Mastering the skill of listening is not nearly as difficult as some would believe. Here are some specific steps you can take to become a better listener immediately!

1. Give the speaker your undivided attention. When you make eye contact and focus on your mate, you're saying, "You are important to me. Your words and ideas have meaning in my life." When you read the paper at the breakfast or dinner table, look around the room, continue watching a television program (or change channels with the remote control), or "doodle" while your mate speaks, you send a very different message. It's simply wise to listen carefully and from time to time nod your head or inject a word or thought to make absolutely certain your mate understands that you are giving him or her your undivided attention.

2. Show your attentiveness with your body language. Sit up and lean forward when talking with your mate. If your manager or the President of the United States were to visit with you, your posture would be different than it often is with your spouse. Why? Your mate will, over the years, have a much greater meaning in your life than *anyone* else. Don't "slight" him or her because of familiarity. Do show respect by being a "well positioned" listener.

3. Rephrase or restate key statements. If you will feed back what you think you are hearing, in your own words, you will show an interest, and you will increase understanding. Use phrases like, "So what I hear you saying is . . ."; "Do you mean to say . . ."; "And that made you feel . . . (angry, happy, sad, glad, etc.)." On those occasions when either of you is frustrated and has a tendency to unload in an impetuous, impatient, dogmatic way, it's certainly a sign of maturity if the other person will quietly say, "I can understand why you're so upset, Sweetheart. Johnny forgot that he had been potty trained and not only ended up with dirty pants, but managed to soil the rug, the bedspread, and the bath mat. And you already had more to do than any two people could handle. Most of all, after all the time you spent on his training, I know how disappointed you must be. No wonder you're so upset!"

Verbalizing the problem clearly shows that you are listening, that you understand and are sympathetic, and that you appreciate all her efforts. Most important, you communicate that even though *things* did not go well, *she* is A-O.K. This approach diffuses a lot of the hurt and anger and preserves her worth as a mother and a person. In most cases, a sympathetic ear, a loving hug, *and* a helping hand will solve the problem of the moment—and firmly implant another brick in the building of love on which your marriage rests.

4. Let your mate finish the sentence. Interrupting with your thoughts or finishing a sentence for your spouse is a fast way to quash communication. Listen—pause—and listen! When you are planning on being married a lifetime, there is plenty of time for you to respond. Listening is just as important as talking. After all, God gave us two ears and only one mouth. We are often guilty of thinking about our next sentence while another person is talking rather than listening carefully to his or her exact words. This is particularly harmful with a spouse. When you're in a conversation with your spouse, try to clear your mind of all your pet personal preferences and prejudices. Make an attempt to view the conversation in the clear light of day. Listen from your mate's frame of reference. What has he been through today? What is her general emotional state? Listen with your ears and your eyes.

5. Express your feelings. One of the most important, and easily the most neglected, components in effective communication involves the simple expressing of feelings. That's sad because in order for real intimacy to develop, partners must be able to express their emotions to one who listens. "Feeling" or "gut level communication" occurs most often with the use of the phrase "I feel . . ." because "I feel" messages convey honest emotions. Incidentally, it's good to be honest about your true emotions, but it's even better to keep them under control. Never say anything derogatory about your mate's character or personality. And eliminate such phrases from your vocabulary as "you never," "you always," "I can't," "you should," and "you shouldn't."

6. Be careful about supplying solutions. Particularly if his wife does not work outside the home, a man may make a fundamental mistake of thinking that when he arrives home in the evening and his wife proceeds to dump part of her frustrations of the day on him, she wants him to play Solomon and give her the benefit of his incredible wisdom. For her, it's been "one of those days." She's been doing battle with an infant and a rambunctious three-year-old, and in his mind she wants him to offer an immediate solution to the problem.

In most instances, that is not the case. She understands that in the majority of these situations there is no immediate solution. What she really wants is an *attentive* ear, a *sympathetic* listener, a *caring* husband, and some *assurance* that she is a good person, a good mother, and a good wife. She's having a little "pity party" that in many cases is well deserved.

One man put it this way: "I was working in a job that required me to quickly, efficiently, and effectively discover answers to problems. That was a real help to me in my job, but a problem in my marriage. When my wife was concerned, harried, upset, or ready to give up on our children, me, herself, or the family pet, the 'world's greatest problem solver' was on the spot with exactly the right answer . . . at exactly the wrong time. Time management, goal setting, appointments to be set, chores to be prioritized, anything and everything she needed was available—except the most important thing of all: SENSITIVITY. She needed a listener, not a talker; she wanted care and concern, not direction. The more my wife failed to heed my words of wisdom, the more I demanded to be heard. My desire to help became a millstone around the neck of our marriage."

Listening is especially important when your mate is frustrated and has had it "up to here." A listening ear, combined with genuine interest and concern and a little hugging, will go a long way in building or rebuilding a relationship.

Listening is loving.

---

7. *Remember: Listening is loving.* A wise man once said that talking is sharing, but listening is caring. For this reason, a wise husband will carefully listen to the woes of the moment and myriads of details and incidents that make up his mate's day. He understands that duty makes us do things well, but love makes us do them beautifully. The exciting thing is that what occasionally starts out as "something you should do" will turn into "something you want to do." Interestingly enough, over a period of time, you will be amazed at how exciting some of those details can be.

THE "HEART" OF LISTENING SKILLS

Good listening is a skill that requires *practice, empathy,* and *true concern* for the other person. There is no greater security you can give your spouse than to carefully listen and verbally encourage with words such as "I know what you mean"; "I understand"; "For goodness sake!"; "You don't mean it!"; "You've got to be kidding!"; "He said WHAT?; "That's great"; "My goodness." Of course, "I love you" will fit into just about any conversation.

IT TAKES TIME TO COMMUNICATE

Amazingly enough, many couples make time for just about everything—and everybody—but each other. I'll have to confess that I am possibly the most guilty person alive on this one, or at least I *was* very guilty. I still am to a degree, but not nearly as much as I was a few years ago. In the past, when acquaintances or business associates would pass through town and say, "It's my only night here," or "I'm just here for the weekend," I would expect my wife to "understand" that I had to see my friend or business associate and that she would have to forget what she had been planning all week. Basically it was a "me-first-and-you-and-the-kids-can-have-what's-left over" approach to marriage. That *is* communication, but unfortunately it's the kind of communication that eliminates any possibility of a loving marriage.

I'm pleased to say that now, in most cases, I have my priorities in order and explain to my business friends that I'd love to get together but prior commitments make it impossible. I will confess that I'm still having to work on turning down some of those intrusions on family time because sometimes they just seem so important. However, in the final analysis, when you make one exception, you'll open the door to rationalizing the second; and as former President Ronald Reagan would say, "There you go again." Now I make appointments with The Redhead, and since my relationship with her is by far the most significant relationship I have, with rare exceptions I keep those appointments. That *communicates*, loudly and clearly, how I really feel about her.

YOU'RE VERY IMPORTANT, BUT I'M BUSY_____

Even as I was writing this chapter on communications, the sound of The Redhead's voice broke my concentration. "Honey, can you come help me with this?"

My first thought was, "Now, she knows I'm in the middle of writing this book on courtship after marriage"—and then before I could finish the thought, the irony caused me to stop and laugh out loud. Isn't it fascinating how we instinctively and instantaneously rate what we are doing as being more important than what our mate is doing?

In this case, what I was doing was clearly the most urgent and important. After all, a book on the family—and specifically on courtship—would rate somewhere in importance between the Bible and *The Decline and Fall of the Roman Empire*. And what was The Redhead doing that was so important she dared interrupt me to ask for my help? Nothing—except wrapping Christmas presents, preparing dinner, and setting the table for this family for which I was so passionately declaring my love (and especially my love for her) in this book.

The first time she will know why I was grinning so big when I responded to her call for help will be when she reads these words in this book. When the impact of my own hypocrisy hit me, I laughed at myself and responded to her call. The "interruption" took all of three minutes (counting the hugging time), and I was "back to the drawing board"—a happier and hopefully wiser and more sensitive husband. By responding to her call for help, I had communicated my love for her and her importance to me.

THIS IS A BIG ONE _____

One of the best and most effective communication steps The Redhead and I have ever taken took place on January 1,

1989. To give you a brief background, let me state that on July 4, 1972, I made my commitment to Jesus Christ. The Redhead had made her commitment much earlier. Beginning January 1, 1989, we took another giant step in our relationship when we each acquired the New International Version of the "One Year Bible." That simply means the Bible is divided into 365 portions and each day's reading includes something from the Old Testament, something from the New, something from Psalms, and something from Proverbs.

Almost without fail, we discuss what we've read that day. If I'm in Dallas, we read the Bible together; and when I'm on the road, we each will have read our Bibles, then we pray together before we discuss the message. It's uncanny how God seems to almost always reveal the same things to each of us from His Word each day. There are also those exciting times when He has shown each one of us something of an entirely different nature than what the other has seen. I can tell you that we feel even closer as a direct result of sharing God's Word on a daily basis.

Over the years I've noticed many times when a particularly moving event takes place in our lives and we are drawn closer and closer to God, we are invariably drawn closer and closer to each other. When you learn to love through Christ, the sweetness of that love is beyond belief, and those communication barriers begin to come down.

COMMUNICATE WITH QUESTIONS AND HUMOR

A sense of humor is critically important if romance and fun are to be permanent parts of the marriage, and humor is a needed ingredient in effective communication. Neither men nor women are attracted to grim, humorless members of the opposite sex. However, we need to make certain our mate thinks that what we say about him or her really is funny and is *not* a put-down in any way. For example, I never tell a joke where my wife is even involved in the scene without clearing it with her first.

Never will I forget one Friday evening when I returned from a tough week on the road. The Redhead met me at the airport, and she was dressed "fit to kill." As usual, she had on some of the good, sweet-smelling stuff that I especially like.

As we were waiting for my bag to come down on the carousel, she snuggled up real close, slipped her hand into mine (she's powerfully friendly, anyhow!), and said, "Honey, I know it's been a long, tough week for you, so if you want to we can stop by the store on the way home and pick up a nice steak or some seafood. While you relax with the paper, I'll prepare a nice dinner for two. Tom is spending the night with Sam, so we'll be by ourselves. Then, Honey, after we've had a nice dinner, I'm certain you won't want to get involved in cleaning dirty dishes and greasy pots and pans, so you can just relax and catch up on some of your reading while I take care of cleaning the kitchen.

"It shouldn't take me more than an hour, hour and a half, two hours at the most. (Pause) Or the thought occurs to me, Honey, that you might be more comfortable and enjoy the evening more if I were completely free to devote all of my time and energy to you. I could do this in a really nice restaurant. Of course, Honey, it's entirely up to you. What do you prefer?" (That Redhead does have a way with words.)

I don't really think it's necessary to tell you we did not stop by the grocery store or cook that dinner at home.*

Not only is humor important and effective in communications, but gentleness, kindness, and thoughtfulness are

---

*From *Secrets of Closing the Sale* (Fleming H. Revell, 1984), reprinted with permission.

also of paramount importance. The guideline for effective communication is for husbands to be just as gentle, kind, and thoughtful in conversations with wives as you are with secretaries or complete strangers who stop you on the street and ask for directions. Wives should be just as thoughtful and considerate of husbands as you are of your coworkers, your employees, or even your hairdresser.

COMMIT—COMMUNICATE—CARE

I want to emphasize that if you practice every communication skill and follow all the suggestions in this book and every other book on the subject, there will still be those occasional miscommunications. In short, I don't believe there is any such thing as a trouble-free marriage with no disagreements. As I said earlier, though, you can disagree without being disagreeable. In our case, The Redhead and I have had, and do have, our difficulties. However, I believe one of the reasons our love has grown through the difficulties, and our marriage is more stable and solid than ever, has to do with the way we have dealt with each other when we disagreed or miscommunicated.

Basically, when we have crossed wires, we have always treated each other with respect. Not once has either of us been vindictive and called the other by some names we would later regret. We've never attacked each other personally, and that's important. We try to remember that failure is an event and not a person, and that we're going to be together a long time. In short, when we made the commitment to marry, we made the commitment to stay together. When we made the commitment to stay together, we knew, as a practical matter, that it would be more fun if we communicated and respected each other. To paraphrase a prophet of old, I encourage you to "*stay* and do thou likewise."

7 | SEX IS NOT A FOUR-LETTER WORD

> Sex is beautiful, delightful, necessary. God made it
> so. It is an expression of oneness, a total
> commitment, a complete self-giving, a sacred
> obligation. Sex is not a right to claim selfishly; not a
> favor to withhold childishly; not a weapon to
> dominate another; not a reward for good behavior.
> —Dr. J. Allan Petersen

I'm sure, if you've read your Bible at all, you're familiar with the following scene. Adam had been alone all of his life, and God could clearly see it was not good for man to be alone. So God put Adam to sleep, performed surgery, removed a portion of his body, and from it created Eve. When Eve stood before Adam, the Bible says Adam looked at her and said, "Bone of my bone and flesh of my flesh." However, Dr. Howard Hendricks of Dallas Theological Seminary says *that* interpretation falls far short of the original Hebrew language (which has a much more literal and accurate translation). I agree with Dr. Hendricks and think you will, too, so read on.

Can you imagine Adam, having been alone all of his life, suddenly being confronted with the most beautiful woman on earth? Yes, I know some of you will say, "She was the *ONLY* woman on earth," and of course, you're right. But not only was she the most beautiful woman of that time, she was the most beautiful woman of all time because God had just created her and God creates only perfection. Now, do you honestly believe that when Adam saw this gorgeous feminine creation standing in front of him, he casually said,

131

"Bone-of-my-bone-and-flesh-of-my-flesh"? You've got to be kidding! The Hebrew translation comes much closer to a loud, wildly enthusiastic, highly motivated, "WOW!"

That's more like it. That's the way Adam saw Eve. I believe that many, many years after we marry, if we keep our marriage in God's hands and follow some commonsense steps and principles, we can keep the "WOW" in the relationship.

SEX WASN'T MAN'S IDEA _____

Some of the "Hollywood types" of today, including the writers of the lurid novels, the editors of some of the risqué magazines, and the producers of an extremely large number of the television shows, try to convey the notion that sex is their idea and a brand-new discovery.

Sex was and is God's idea. He created us; created the attraction between male and female; told us from the beginning that we were to be fruitful and multiply; and made it extremely clear (in both Old and New Testaments) that a sexual relationship between man and wife extended far beyond the procreation of the races. One of the wisest men who ever lived elaborated on this in the Song of Solomon. In the New Testament, Paul made it clear that a sexual relationship is for the enjoyment of husbands and wives and is designed to cement the bond so they become as one.

Sex wasn't _perfected_ by Masters and Johnson or _originally detailed_ in the Kinsey Report. As stated earlier, the sexual relationship between man and woman was God's idea, and the Bible is the finest manual on sex and sexuality ever written.

If you think that's an exaggeration, I challenge you to read the Song of Solomon. I guarantee it will give you a different perspective as Solomon, visually and verbally, describes the process of courting his bride. You see, many in our society, who haven't read the Bible and who certainly don't know the Author, make unsubstantiated claims that a judging God is against sex. Mainstream Christianity clearly sees a sexual relationship between husband and wife as part of God's creation and plan for man's fulfillment.

SEX AND RELIGION

God's intentions as well as the beauty and benefits that come with following God's plan were verified in a study by *Redbook* magazine involving over one hundred thousand women. This study revealed that those women who have the deepest religious commitments are the happiest in their sexual relationships with their husbands.

This proves yet again the fact that when God gives us rules to live by, He does so not because He is a restrictive, non-caring, unloving God, but because He is *love* and wants the absolute best for us. As you read the Song of Solomon and listen to the intimacy of the relationship between Solomon and his bride, you will hear loudly and clearly that the sexual relationship between man and wife is ordained by God and can be—should be—a loving, satisfying relationship. This is not to imply that a healthy sexual relationship is the most vital aspect of our lives as husband and wives because study after study proves otherwise. But those who have successful, lasting marriages know that physical intimacy is very important, beautiful, and sacred.

As Dr. David Seamands observes, "The notion that Christians are repressed and Victorian is a myth. The fact is that a Christian marriage provides the security that couples need for maximum sexual freedom and enjoyment."

My own research definitely reveals that even the Puritans, despite their reputation, were far more affectionate and loving than they were pictured in our history books. Actually, they were relatively positive about sexuality, since they had a warm understanding of the value of family life.

PHYSICAL INTIMACY

The sexual relationship is a significant part of marriage and the courtship after marriage concept. The physical closeness shared by two people committed to each other for life in the "loving bonds" of holy matrimony can be by far the most intimate and exciting phase of a healthy marriage. The truly sacred, beautiful, and holy act of sharing yourself completely with your mate brings marriage partners together more closely and lovingly than any other event.

Tragically, many husbands and wives use their sexual relationship in a selfish, non-loving manner. Instead, husbands and wives must seek to find fulfillment in this most special of all marital relationships.

The primary sexual organ is the brain.

The reason husbands and wives have problems in the sexual relationship has less to do with the physical act of sex and more to do with the malfunction of the primary sexual organ. Now, you obviously know that I am referring to the brain. Too many people have too many misconceptions about intimacy in marriage. We begin to clear up the confusion when we understand that the sexual relationship does not start in the bedroom *after* the lights go out. That relationship is part of all of life and starts *anew each day* in the bedroom when we awaken and turn those lights on. If your sexual relationship with your mate isn't everything you want it to be, the "problem" in *most* cases is not the "sexual" relationship but "THE" relationship. You must clearly understand that AFFECTION, INTIMACY, KINDNESS, and CONSIDERATION are the important components of your relationship.

Affection, intimacy, kindness, and consideration are important components of every relationship.

SEX IN EVERY ROOM

Let's look at what you can do from the front steps through the back door with stops in every room in the house.

The front door area (foyer) is where you greet your mate when you depart and return to start and end the workday. Since the first and last greetings divide periods of separation, you must work to keep this area a "happy spot." Smiles, hugs, kind words, and positive encouragement are the order of the day (and night).

The kitchen is an area for closeness. If the cliche, "The way to a man's heart is through his stomach," has any truth, then the kitchen can be very important to the marriage. Men who help their wives in the kitchen are more respected and appreciated in other rooms of the home.

The dining room is an excellent area for communication and spiritual growth. Prayer before meals draws everyone closer. Discussing the positive aspects of the day (leave the negative for after the meal) will not only increase communication but also help digestion.

The den or family room is the place to relax and let your "hair down." The family room filled with conversation that is spiced with laughter helps build the marriage. This is also the room your son and/or daughter should spend some time in getting to know a future spouse during the dating process.

When all the rooms of the home are used properly, the bedroom becomes a beautiful, exciting, and loving room!

PAY ATTENTION, MEN!

You will notice that much of this chapter is aimed at husbands. There are two reasons for this. *Tons* of mail to "Ann Landers" and "Dear Abby," as well as countless studies, clearly establish that in most cases the husband is the aggressive one. That's O.K. and true to his nature. But, husbands, please remember that affection, love, tenderness, and consideration must be the bed upon which that assertiveness rests.

Second, both husband and wife need to know that for the sexual relationship to be beautiful and satisfying, both must feel loved and not used. As many of you have come to know, the sex drive for you and your spouse will vary considerably. That's where genuine love, concern, consideration, and communication become of paramount importance. Loving, understanding, and keeping your mate's needs and desires foremost will ultimately lead not only to a win-win relationship but a permanently happy one as well. Now, let's take a careful look at how we can make our "bedroom marriage" consistent with the other aspects of our marriage.

WHERE DOES SEX BEGIN?

The basic problem in most sexual relationships in marriage is that too many husbands and wives see the sexual relationship (or at least they *treat* the sexual relationship) as a separate or independent part of their lives. That's a serious mistake.

Gentlemen, I can tell you with absolute certainty that when you ignore your wife all day long (and on occasion are even thoughtless and inconsiderate or downright rude and demanding) and then proceed to give her your undivided attention when the lights go out, your wife resents it. It's also true that if you gripe about the mashed potatoes (or lack of them) at dinner, all you're gonna get the rest of the evening is cold shoulder.

Ladies, I can tell you with absolute certainty that when you ignore your husband's efforts (though they may be "clumsy") to "set the stage" for intimacy, he resents it. By withholding physical affection, you reduce the likelihood of those "tender moments" that can fall before and after the act of lovemaking.

Sexual intercourse between husband and wife is the "ultimate" in a relationship, but far too many men, because of our very nature and sometimes lack of sensitivity, make the mistake of trying to go from the evening news to the "ultimate" with nothing but a change of clothing or a shedding of clothes in between. Far too many women are caught up in the "tyranny of the urgent" (the stress of home, work, and children) and simply are not "in the mood" on far too many occasions. At times that's natural and understandable, but as a steady diet, it adds up to an unfortunate, even tragic, case of malnutrition.

The wife who is asked to meet her husband's needs and desires with no consideration of her needs and desires will feel used and eventually will feel like little more than a prostitute. That "ain't" the way to achieve wedded bliss, fellows. You must meet her needs if the ultimate is to be reached in your marriage. The husband who is regularly rejected with little or no attention given to his needs and desires will feel less of a man because, according to psychologists, sexual rejection is *complete* rejection to men. That "ain't" the way to achieve wedded bliss, ladies. You must meet his needs if the ultimate is to be reached in your marriage.

All of us want to be romanced and courted as we were before the wedding bells rang. We want to be—must be— made to feel loved, needed, and appreciated if we are going to be truly responsive sexually over the years. In order for the sexual relationship to reach the zenith and enable husband and wife to become the "one" God intended, courtship in the truest sense must include time, attention, affection, and thoughtfulness. This is especially true after the first few years when the honeymoon becomes a dim memory.

I'M PROUD OF YOU, HONEY_____

We men and women are absolutely amazing! Before we get married we smother each other with attention, shower each other with calls, and make absolutely certain that we spend every possible waking moment with our chosen one. Then, when we get married, that seems to change over a period of time. I've noticed on many occasions at a social event that husband and wife arrive together and immediately go their separate ways. They scarcely know the other is in existence until they are ready to make their departure. I'm not saying you should spend every moment with each other, but by and large, when you're invited as a couple, both of you will enjoy the social event more and will grow closer together if you spend the majority of your time together. That's the way you build friendships with other couples while being identified as having a solid, "together" marriage.

Think back to that time, men, when you were in the early stages of courting. You took *HER!* to the big social, and if some lecherous male made the mistake of approaching, you boldly stepped forward and stood between him and *HER!* so you could ward off his advances. And for the rest of the evening, the two of you were as close as Siamese twins. The greatest compliment you can pay your bride, regardless of how long you've been married, is to continue to treat her the same way. When you go to those events together, whether it's a party, an athletic event, a dinner out, or a charity event, the time you spend together publicly can make a major difference in your marriage. The message you deliver is clear: "I love my mate, I'm proud of my mate, and I want the world *and* my mate to know it!" Then when you get home and tell your wife how much you love her, the believability factor is strong because you've been demonstrating that love *all* evening.

IT TAKES TIME

Despite the beauty, joy, and excitement of a sexual relationship between husband and wife, a study by New York psychiatrist Anthony Pietropinto found that one-third of all married couples under the age of forty-five had, at some point, ceased sexual relations altogether for a period of at least two months. According to Pietropinto, this decline in sexual activity can be directly attributed to a rise in job-related stress, particularly among two-career couples. His assessment: "Sex is a function that requires a certain amount of attention, affection and effort. People typically need to get psychologically prepared for it, which isn't easy if someone is tired from a day's work."

Combine this with another recent study showing that not only do two-career couples spend less time together, but the time they do spend together is not satisfying. Therefore, we can easily conclude that one of the most important ingredients for successful sexual relations within marriage is time. T-I-M-E. In fact, as I read the Song of Solomon, I am impressed with the fact that this busy man—who governed his kingdom and had an interest in art, architecture, construction, horticulture, and all sorts of other fields— apparently spent a great deal of time courting his beautiful bride. Why? I believe, God saw fit for him to record, in poetic fashion, the details of his courting to show us that sex and courtship in marriage have not only *His* approval but *His* encouragement.

One of the saddest stories I have ever heard concerned a divorced couple. When asked by a friend how she was dealing with her recent divorce, the spurned wife replied, "Better than expected; I get more of John's time and attention now than before. I finally got on his 'To Do' list." How frustrating to think of what might have been had this couple planned and kept the most important time commitment of all—the time promised to love, honor, and cherish each other.

CREATING AN INTEREST IN SEX

One of the ironies of life, men, is the fact that husbands can get wives interested in a sexual relationship by not talking about sex at all. Most "affairs" occur not because the object of attention is so strikingly beautiful or devilishly handsome, but because that person perceived another was interested in him or her as a "person." When you "court" your wife as a way of life, show her genuine respect and affection, become deeply interested in her, and spend *time* with her, then the sexual aspect of your marriage becomes the natural course of action.

Surely you remember all the plotting and maneuvering you did to get your beloved off by herself before you got married. You didn't want to just be with your one and only; you wanted to be *alone* with her. I won't accuse you of doing that so you could seduce her, but the odds are pretty good that you had plans for being "friendlier" with her if you were alone than if you were in a small group.

At this point in your relationship, you may not think in terms of "seducing" your wife, but the same careful planning, with the same excitement and thoughtfulness, will set the stage for you to come together in "oneness."

PLEASURE AND FIDELITY

Please notice that you can enjoy the pleasure of sex with your mate indefinitely and happiness is a natural by-product. Infidelity might, for a season, produce pleasure, but in 100 percent of the cases it eventually destroys happiness and produces misery for the pleasure-seeking, self-centered people involved as well as the innocent members of all the families.

ACHIEVING THE ULTIMATE

By now it has become obvious (if it wasn't before) that the man and the woman must accept equal responsibility for the sexual success of the relationship. If you are willing to accept your portion of the responsibility, you will want to know the specifics of what can be done to "achieve the ultimate." The rest of this chapter is designed to share ideas you can use to improve a poor sexual relationship or make a great one even better. Since many people who are basically good, but nevertheless subject to temptation and the weaknesses of the flesh, fall prey to sexual relationships outside marriage, I hope you will carefully read and ponder the following thoughts.

Step One: Avoid Prolonged Absences

In our society today, there are many men—and an increasingly large number of women—who have traveling jobs that take them away from their families for extended periods of time. In most cases, prolonged absences simply do not help solidify marriage. So, to achieve the ultimate in mutual sexual satisfaction, you must avoid prolonged absences.

Over a period of years, when a mate is gone from Monday through Friday or in some cases, two, three, or four weeks at a time, a strain is placed on the relationship that makes it very difficult for the marriage to survive. The reality is, with extended absences, you've got to wonder if there really is a marriage. Perhaps I relate too much to my own situation, but I know that if I were gone on a consistent basis for the entire week or longer periods of time, I fear my own relationship with The Redhead would seriously deteriorate. Combine this with the fact that in my travels I've seen many, many instances of infidelity and I know of countless marriages that have been destroyed because of constant and prolonged separations.

Since many of you who are reading this undoubtedly know that I travel a great deal, you might wonder where I fit in this category. To begin with, I'm always home over the weekend. Second, I generally leave on Monday evening or Tuesday morning, and in 98 percent of the cases, I'm home by Friday. In about 40 percent of the cases, I'm home on Wednesday, leaving on Thursday and coming back on Friday. In addition, we do six three-day seminars in Dallas each year, and I am home all week on those occasions. I also set aside five weeks each year for writing, which I do at home, and I take two weeks in the summer and two weeks at Christmas for vacation and family time. Bottom line: I spend less than one hundred nights each year away from home, and on about ten of those nights, The Redhead is with me. With careful planning, you can control prolonged absences. Two basic questions: Is the standard of living provided by your absenteeism more important than your marriage?

What would an objective look at your calendar reveal about your priorities in life?

It is very important that separations not be very long. In *The Everyday Bible* (which is written at the third-grade, ninth-month level) Paul spells out why in simple detail in 1 Corinthians 7:2–5:

> But sexual sin is a danger. So each man should have his own wife. And each woman should have her own husband. The husband should give his wife all that she should have as his wife. And the wife should give her husband all that he should have as her husband. The wife does not have power over her own body. Her husband has the power over her body. And the husband does not have power over his own body. His wife has the power over his body. Do not refuse to give your bodies to each other. But you might both agree to stay away from sexual relations for a time. You might do this so that you can give your time to prayer. Then come together again. This is so that Satan cannot tempt you in your weakness.

Step Two: Get Physical Without Being Sensual

A pat on the shoulder, a touch of the hand, a hug, a quick kiss on the cheek—all these physical actions that say "I love you" without saying "let's go to bed" have a profound impact on our sexual relationships. Ladies, when you reach for your husband's hand or give him a hug, you are saying, "You are mine, and I am yours." Men, when we share a kiss on the cheek or a hug for the sake of a hug—without sexual overtones—we are helping our wives know that our love goes beyond the physical relationship.

Men and women who don't hug a lot just for the joy of hugging miss out on much of the sheer joy of marriage. I'll have to confess that I hit the jackpot in the hugging department because The Redhead is in a class apart in that area. As a matter of fact, she is affectionately known as "The Happy

Hugger." As Miss Mamie McCullough would say, "If it's moving, she'll stop it and hug it, and if it's not, she'll dust it off and sell it."

In a typical day, when I'm around the house doing my work, The Redhead and I will hug from a dozen times to as many as thirty or forty times. They're not lengthy, suggestive, or passionate; they simply reaffirm our love for each other. They say, "I'm so glad you're mine and I am yours. I'm delighted to have you around. You mean so much to me. What a privilege it is to have exclusivity with you."

Gentlemen, when you do a lot of hugging with your wife, when hugging is all you're interested in, you are communicating your love in a special way. You are also setting the stage for the sexual relationship. You're clearly saying, "I love you," and your wife will feel loved and not used. Then when that love is culminated with the sexual experience, it is simply highlighting the depth of the love and the spirit of oneness between a man and his wife. Based on the impact "The Happy Hugger" has had on my life, I agree with all the studies and observations documenting scientifically that hugging helps in virtually every area of life. Hugging has definitely helped me become the kind of positive optimist I'm notorious for being. Now, let's look at another "little thing" that will be a big plus in a relationship.

Step Three: Start the Day Lovingly

One little thing you can do to create a courtship environment for a permanent marriage is to get up a few minutes earlier each day. You can use those first few minutes to adjust to each other, to get in a couple of wake-up hugs, and to profess your love for each other. Spend a few minutes holding hands, and enjoy a quiet cup of coffee before the hustle and bustle of the day start. Even fifteen minutes can make quite a difference. Thought: *Millions* of people get up early to prepare for their jobs and professions so they can be more effective and move ahead faster. Since career success is directly tied to marital success, doesn't it make sense to give your marriage first priority as you start the day?

After that pleasant start, you work much better together as a team getting the children up and ready for school. When you leave for work, you kiss each other good-bye—not like you're brother and sister, but like you're bride and groom! As we'd say down home, "You really leave your wife well-kissed; you flat strop it on 'er!" The reason is simple. Research by a West German insurance company reveals that a man who kisses his wife good-bye—I mean *really* kisses her good-bye—will live an average of five and one-half years longer than do those men who forgo this pleasant little interlude. Fellows, your life is at stake! Not only that, but the men who do this earn an average of 20 to 30 percent more money than do those who have to leave home under their own power; so, yes, there are lots of benefits for both sides.

Step Four: Greet Each Other Positively

If both husband and wife work and arrive home together at or about the same time, when you greet each other, it should be with a hug and a friendly greeting, "It's good to see you," and then you should spend the next few minutes in some very positive affirmations. (That helps to create a positive, loving environment.)

You *never* greet each other with gripes, complaints, and fussing. You don't complain about the weather, the smog, the impossible traffic conditions, or "Let me tell you about that dummy down at the office or at the plant." Many times husbands and wives try to outdo each other as they go into the lurid details about what a miserable day they had, what a miserable place they work in, what a miserable company, what a miserable boss, etc. (I guarantee you, that's a sexual turnoff.)

After the pleasantries of hugging and holding hands for

a minute, each claiming delight at seeing the other, you need to ask for or volunteer some exciting, interesting, or entertaining information. "Let me tell you about something funny that happened down at the office." Or "Let me tell you about something really neat that happened to me." Or "Do you want to go first and tell me about the most fun thing you did all day?" In short, when you make that reentry, it should be a definite plus, a positive one. (A smiling mate is more attractive than a frowning one.)

When you do this over a period of time, you set up a positive expectancy on both parts, and you begin to wonder what the good news will be today. You know it's going to be exciting to see your mate because you know something exciting has been happening. On the other hand, if you greet each other with gripes and complaints, you start associating getting back together with a negative. That's when you need to be aware of the fact that the chances of a stop at the local bar (seems like more fun than a grouchy mate) for a couple of "cool ones" could easily get to be the order of the day. It doesn't take much of that kind of conduct to destroy a marriage.

Greeting each other positively does not deny the reality of life; it simply keeps things in proper order. After dinner, when things are settled down and you're not tense from the job or traffic, that's the time to discuss your concerns or problems. You will be more relaxed, more comfortable, and more receptive. And as you empathetically share those problems *and* creatively work to solve them, you will be drawn closer and more lovingly together.

Try This One, Ladies

At the end of the day, if the wife is not working or if she has gotten home before her husband, I encourage you, ladies, to plan for his arrival. *Don't* call out from the back of the house as you hear the front door open with a loud, "Is that you, Honey!?" *Do* go to the front door, make certain it is "Honey," and let him know that you are delighted to see him, that you are glad he is home.

I encourage you to remember, ladies, that all day he's been around women who have been putting and keeping their best foot forward. They have been dressed neatly and, in most cases, quite tastefully and probably have had on a reasonable amount of perfume and makeup so that they will be their most attractive. I also encourage you to remember that 50 percent of all divorces are caused by a mate who met someone else in the workplace and 70 percent of the time it is somebody who works in close proximity to the mate.

I mention this not to have you grill your husband every evening when he comes in—and certainly not to give you any undue concern—but only to encourage you to make certain that when he gets home, he is met by the friendliest, best-smelling, prettiest girl he's seen all day. (Remember, men are sight oriented.) Then when you greet him at the front door, he truly will be elated to see you, and your exuberance will have him looking forward to coming straight home every day.

And let's not forget the old sauce for the goose, sauce for the gander routine, fellows. If she works outside the home, she, too, has been around men all day, and they were neat and well dressed. They, too, in many cases, had their best foot forward and treated your wife with courtesy and respect. They probably had used some clean-smelling cologne or after-shave lotion. *SO* if you get home before your wife, a little cleanup job on you would be helpful. She will be especially impressed if you get the evening routine started. (Feed the dog, let the cat out, make the coffee, dry the clothes she put in the washer that morning, etc.) This "little thing" clearly communicates to your wife that you not only love her but want to function as a full-fledged team member and ease her burden as much as possible.

Step Five: Meet Your Mate's "Special Occasion" Needs

And now a special note to the wife: When on occasion, a man's ego has been shattered and his self-image destroyed, a special amount of T.L.C. is needed from you. For example, if he has lost his job or been disappointed in a business venture, you become "especially" important to him at this time. If that should ever happen in your marriage, I encourage you to become more aggressive in seeking a sexual relationship with your mate. Nothing will reassure him as much as the knowledge that his wife finds him sexually attractive. He can be shattered with rejection after rejection or blown away by being passed over for a well-deserved promotion. However, when he comes home, if you make his importance to you very clear and show your love for him and the fact that you find him sexually attractive, it will do more for his ego and confidence than any other single thing.

Husbands, the same sensitivity should be applied in the way you deal with your wife. If her ego has been damaged and her image and confidence are suffering, your affection and understanding can do much to restore her confidence and build a long, lasting relationship. Caution: Her need, in most cases, is for you to hug, hold, listen, be empathetic and understanding. Unless she makes it crystal clear that she is interested in you sexually, you should be anything but aggressive with her, or she could feel "used" and taken advantage of instead of loved and comforted.

Heaven on Earth

Certainly cultivating the relationship by courting each other is very essential, and taking the time to do so is a priority. In fact, when I sat down some years ago to talk with my son about the dangers of premarital sex—and there are a number of major dangers—conversation came around to marriage and to his mother and me. He thrilled me to no end when he told me that his idea of heaven on earth was associated with watching us take off every year for the three days we always set aside for just each other to celebrate our wedding anniversary. The truth is, that's my idea of heaven on earth, too. As stated earlier, I'm very much in love with The Redhead, and my heart still skips a beat when I see her after we've been apart for even a short time. I find her to be the most fascinating and excitingly beautiful woman I've ever known.

Now, many times you'll be watching television and see the advertisement, "Most beautiful love story ever told." Well, those advertisers could be right, but they will only be the most beautiful love stories ever *told*. They won't be the most beautiful love stories ever because the most beautiful love stories ever will never be told. No man and woman, deeply committed to each other in the bonds of holy matrimony, would ever reveal the intimacies of their love. To do so would make their love common, and nothing common is really beautiful.

Step Six: Remember God's Plan

Finally, we need to remember that according to God's own wisdom and design, sexuality was part of the plan. After all, "He made them male and female." He designed this means for the propagation of the race and for a pleasurable expression of the kind of love between man and wife that can nourish true oneness. The Bible often uses the Hebrew word "to know" to describe the sexual love experience of husband and wife. Knowing means far more than objective information and intellectual recognition of a person. It means a mutual exchange of the deepest sort of knowledge possible about the loved one.

As a result, neither the distorted image of negative Puritanism nor the so-called new morality that advocates removing all sexual restraints gives us an accurate picture of God's good gift of sex. He gave the sexual relationship to husbands and wives to be enjoyed as an ultimately exhilarating part of a committed marriage relationship.

READ ALL ABOUT IT

I encourage you to get a copy of Dr. Ed Wheat's book, *Intended For Pleasure*. Dr. Wheat is a physician with an enormous amount of medical and counseling experience combined with a solid spiritual base from which he operates. This book is beautifully and tastefully written, and yet, it is graphic and very specific in suggestions and instructions. Many, many times frustrations and even pain are brought about because of some very solvable problems. This is not to imply that the solution will be easy, but the reality is that many frustrating and completely unsatisfactory sexual relationships have, through Dr. Wheat's counseling and information, been brought to a point of complete enjoyment and even exhilaration with a far deeper and more satisfying marriage as the result.

The second book that I really encourage you to dig into is *The Act of Marriage* by Tim and Beverly LaHaye. They deal with virtually every aspect of the relationship and most specifically and intimately with the sexual aspect of the marriage. In this book you have the added advantage of looking at it from both the male and the female perspectives so that you know how the relationship affects both husband and wife and what can be done to bring that relationship to the bedroom in a very intimate and beautiful way.

And as I have mentioned previously, Dr. Richard Furman's book, *The Intimate Husband,* contains some beautiful guidelines to build the proper, loving relationship.

There are several other excellent books listed in the Bibliography.

Again, I believe that God intended for the sexual relationship to be a beautiful, exciting, and rewarding one for both husband and wife. Surely any man or woman who is married would want his or her partner to receive the maximum enjoyment from one of God's special gifts to us. Pick up one or all three of these books, and I believe your relationship can be far richer and better.

Incidentally, I might also add that for those of you who currently have a beautiful sexual relationship, the relationship could well be improved beyond what you already enjoy with the information contained in these books.

THE BOTTOM LINE

To be completely candid at this point, there are many of you reading this book who do not enjoy as good a sexual relationship with your mate as you might. This could be caused by a number of factors, but in virtually every case, there is a solution. I recognize that many of you have tried many of those solutions, but I'm convinced that if you will put the *entire contents* of this book to work, you will find your answers. Your sexual relationship is affected by *all* facets of your relationship, so to make the weak strong, or the great even greater, live fully in all the rooms of your home and the bedroom will take care of itself.

8 | WHO WEARS THE PANTS? OR LEADERSHIP VS. DICTATORSHIP

> God took woman from man's side for a purpose.
> Not from his head, so that she might lord over him,
> or from his feet, so that he could trample on her,
> but rather from his side, from underneath the
> protective position of his arm, so they could walk
> side by side down life's highway.
>
> —Anonymous

Norman Vincent Peale tells of visiting a building site with the mayor of one of America's great cities. Dr. Peale's wife, Ruth, and the mayor's wife accompanied the two men as they toured the construction site.

As the party approached a group of workmen, one of the men called out to the mayor's wife, asking if she remembered him. She acknowledged that she did, and the two chatted briefly, revealing that the construction worker was an old flame of twenty years before. Finally the party moved on their way. With a smug look, the mayor declared, "Well, my dear, if you had married him, you would be the wife of a construction worker." "On the contrary, Dear," replied his wife. "If I had married him, he would be the mayor."*

LEADERSHIP

Nowhere in this book is there a greater opportunity for us to disagree than in this chapter because I am dealing with

---

*From *How to Conquer Problems* (Positive Communications, Inc., 70 Route 22, Pawling, NY 12564), used with permission.

> **"Godly wisdom and love, in the truest sense, lead men and women to recognize each other's strengths and allow these strengths to be used to solidify the relationship."**
> **—Victor Oliver**

one of the most misinterpreted issues in marriage—the leadership role. I began the chapter with Dr. Peale's story because MUTUALITY is a key concept in understanding any leadership role. As my friend Victor Oliver says: "Godly wisdom and love, in the truest sense, lead men and women to recognize each other's strengths and allow these strengths to be used to solidify the relationship."

There are many "arenas" of life where one spouse has a great strength but the other spouse has a great weakness. Leadership means identifying strengths and weaknesses, agreeing on responsibilities in these areas, and having regular times of evaluation to "inspect to make sure you get what you expect."

> **"Leadership is not making all the decisions; leadership is seeing to it that the right person is making the decisions."**
> **—Jim Savage**

Finances and child-rearing are two of the most volatile areas for consideration. I could cite many examples of families where the woman has greater ability than the man in

"Inspect to make sure you get what you expect."
—Zig Ziglar

these areas . . . and vice versa. The key is recognition of strengths.

Leadership is not making all the decisions. Leadership sees to it that the right person is making the decisions.

TEAMWORK

Now, let's dig a little deeper and look at some things husbands and wives can do in order to function more effectively as a team. As a young salesman, I had the privilege of being trained by a dedicated man who was much like an older brother. His name was Bill Cranford, and he has the proverbial patience of Job, which certainly helped in dealing with this struggling, inept, young non-producer.

When I finally learned to survive in the world of selling and started to move up in management, Bill taught me an important, yet very simple lesson in leadership. One day he took a piece of string and said, "Zig, this piece of string would be tough to push, but it's easy to pull. People are pretty much that way—easy to lead, but hard to push. As you move up into management, Zig, you'll discover that if you'll set the example and provide the leadership for your people, you won't have to do much pushing. They'll be delighted to follow the leader."

From my experience over the years in the business world as well as in the home, I can tell you Bill was right. This is true in sales, business, church, and politics, and it's especially true in the family.

Speaking of leading by example, one of the best practitioners of that art was Benjamin Franklin. Convinced that the city of Philadelphia needed street lights, Franklin knew that example would be more persuasive than any argument he could present. With that in mind, he devised a unique method of convincing his neighbors that Philadelphia should have street lights. One day he hung a handsome lantern on a long bracket outside his own door. He kept the lantern brass beautifully polished and the wick carefully trimmed.

Before long, Franklin's neighbors began placing lanterns outside their own doors. Soon the citizens of Philadelphia were ready to light their streets.

Edgar A. Guest once proclaimed, "I'd rather see a sermon than hear one any day." He was right, and yet many husbands still try to lead through proclamation instead of loving example.

Leaders are sorely needed, but in the home, as in life, there's also an important case to be made for followers. S. I. McMillen, in his book _None of These Diseases_, tells a story of a young woman who wanted to go to college, but her heart sank when she read the question on the application blank that asked, "Are you a leader?" Being both honest and conscientious, she wrote, "No," and returned the application, expecting the worst.

To her surprise, she received this letter from the college: "Dear Applicant: A study of the application forms reveals that this year our college will have 1,452 new leaders. We are accepting you because we feel it is imperative that they have at least _one_ follower."

WHO'S THE BOSS?

Followers need leaders, and every organization, team, or family needs someone who is in charge. Any organization without a person who has the authority to make the final decision is going to be leaderless and not accomplish its major objectives. An athletic team needs a captain or quarterback. Every business or military unit must have a CEO or commander in chief and a chain of command in order for the unit to function smoothly. The family is no exception. God identifies that chain of command in the first (and finest) manual on marriage ever written.

First Corinthians 11:3 says, "Now I want you to realize that the head of every man is Christ, and the head of the woman is man, and the head of Christ is God" (NIV).

Notice the order of the chain of command. Christ is to be the head of the man. This is first and foremost, and if it is broken here, then the rest of the chain cannot hold. Notice that just as Christ submits to God, so must the husband submit to Christ. Amazingly enough, many husbands arrogantly and dogmatically claim their "rights" as "boss" without accepting the responsibility and clear instructions to submit. The husband's real focus, as author Dennis Rainey suggests, should be on *how* he should lead and not on how his wife should submit. (Please reread this last paragraph very carefully.)

DANGEROUS SEMANTICS

Since language and the meaning of words often change over the years, many people get "all shook up" when they read words like *submit* and/or *submissive*. To begin with, *submit* is not a word that means the individual who submits becomes a non-person or gives up all rights or responsibilities or that the person always agrees. In fact, it was a word used in the Roman military to describe the relationship between a colonel and a general. The general had ultimate responsibility. The colonel had responsibility and was a highly respected individual, yet, he deferred overall on ultimate authority to the general. Christ is general to the man's colonel.

In the same way, in the field of business, every company has a CEO, but most companies and organizations will have numerous executives, *all* of whom make important decisions. For example, in our company, we have a CEO, but we also have a senior vice president, a vice president, and several other high-level managers, all of whom have areas in which they are responsible and maintain authority. They have considerable input and influence in many areas concerning the overall operation of the company, based on their strengths. In fact, in our company, all major management decisions are arrived at through interaction and in-depth discussion by the senior executives. However, if agreement cannot be achieved, then we have a decision-maker, our CEO—the final decision, of necessity, is made by him.

My friend, Dr. Paul Meier, who is not only a psychiatrist and marriage counselor, but the executive vice president of his organization, the Minirth-Meier Clinics, explains the "chain of command" in the home as follows:

> In our marriage, because of what the Bible says, I'm the president and my wife is the executive vice president. Usually we agree. If we don't agree, we talk things out together. On the rare instances where we can't resolve our disagreements over an issue by talking it out, it's my responsibility to make the final call.
>
> In the same way, in our Minirth-Meier Clinic, Frank, my partner, is the president and I'm the executive vice president. We approach things, in a sense, on a 50-50 basis. His 50 is just a shade heavier than mine, though.

First Peter 3:1 reinforces this concept and gives a beautiful reason *why* this order is established: "Wives, in the same way be submissive to your husbands so that, if any of them do not believe the word, they may be won over without words by the behavior of their wives" (NIV).

THE "WEAKER" PARTNER

First Peter 3:7 clearly spells out the husband's role and responsibility: "Husbands, in the same way be considerate as you live with your wives, and treat them with respect as the weaker partner and as heirs with you of the gracious gift of life, so that nothing will hinder your prayers" (NIV). He is to be considerate of his wife. This means that he is to be thoughtful and observant of her rights and needs, sensitive to her feelings, respectful of her intelligence and the contribution she makes to his life, to the Kingdom, and to the family. As I said earlier, nothing is so strong as gentleness; nothing so gentle as real strength.

The second part of the verse creates problems for some people because of the use of the term *weaker partner*. However, an understanding of what the words mean in the original language and context brings smiles and not frowns to the face and heart of the reader. First, *weaker* certainly does not mean the "lesser" partner. In the original language, the terminology referred to "kinder, gentler, more loving, more delicate, finer, more complex, gracious, and empathetic." I think you will agree that those are not characteristics of a *lesser* partner.

Since the word *weaker* does disturb some people today, let me share with you the way God taught me the definition. Several years ago, my wife, son, and I were on a trip from Dallas to Mississippi. As we drove along, we needed gasoline, so I pulled into a service station. I filled up, paid my bill, and was pulling out when I noticed two men sitting next to a refreshment center, leaning up against one of the cold drink boxes. They were shabbily dressed, had obviously neither shaved nor bathed in a number of days, and looked quite unkempt. As we drove past, in my kind, gentle thoughtful, and loving way, I muttered under my breath, "Couple of bums! They ought to get 'em a job and go to work!" The Redhead looked at me in some small amount of shock and quietly said, "Honey, those men might be hungry. They're obviously down on their luck, which can happen to anybody. They need our prayers and help, not our judgment and criticism." I stood corrected! The more I think about it, the more I know that's the kind of person I want by my side all my life. She "completes" me, and hopefully, I "complete" her.

I actually don't believe that I am generally as critical or judgmental of my fellowman as I was of those two hitchhikers. I relate the incident because I think it clearly spells out an essential difference between the man and the woman. Women *are* gentler, more thoughtful, compassionate, considerate, and loving, and I, for one, am elated that they are.

The verse, 1 Peter 3:7, further says that your wife is an heir with you of the gracious gift of life. The summation of the last part of the verse, "so that nothing will hinder your prayers," should put every husband in the world on his best, kindest, and most considerate behavior. The message is crystal clear that if we do not deal with our wives properly, we can forget our prayer life because God simply is not going to hear us.

In his book, *Lonely Husbands, Lonely Wives*, Dennis Rainey points out that the Greek word used in the New Testament for submission is *hypotasso*, which means "to voluntarily complete, arrange, adapt, or blend so as to make a complete whole or complete pattern." In short, the wife voluntarily submits, and the wise husband graciously accepts and then fills the leadership position God has designated him for. *That* is his opportunity *and* responsibility.

BE A CHEERLEADER

As the executive vice president of our family, The Redhead has been my number one cheerleader and my greatest encourager. As I mentioned in chapter 1, for the first twenty-seven years of our marriage, I was never able to give her financial security. Now that doesn't mean we were broke for twenty-seven years, but it does mean we had plenty of ups and downs. In fact, I was truly a "wandering generality." Yet, in all of those years, not once did I ever hear The Redhead say, "If we just had a little more money, here's what we could do." Instead, it was always, "Honey, you've got what it takes; tomorrow's going to be better."

Ladies, there's no way on earth I can tell you what it meant to me, all those years, to have a cheerleader cheering me on every day of my life and praying for me every night. Men, there's no way I can tell you what it will mean to your wife personally and to your relationship with your wife if you will become her cheerleader, prayer partner, and encourager. When she truly understands how important she is to you, that you want her *and* need her, then you are building a base for happiness *and* stability.

In 1849 when Nathaniel Hawthorne was dismissed from his government job in the customshouse, he went home in despair. His wife listened to his tale of woe, sat pen and ink on the table before him, lit the fire, put her arms around his shoulders, and said, "Now you will be able to write your novel." Hawthorne did, and the result was that classic *The Scarlet Letter*.

F. W. Herzberger tells of a time in Martin Luther's life when life was the gloomiest.

It seems at one point, Luther was extremely depressed, refused to eat and drink, would not speak to his anxious wife, his children or friends.

At the point of his deepest gloom, his wife Catherine put on widow's garments and began to assume the position of a person in deepest mourning.

Surprised, Luther asked, "Why are you sorrowing?"

To which his wife, Kathy, replied, "Dear doctor, I have cause for the saddest of weeping, for God in his heaven has died."

This gentlest of rebuke did not fail Luther. With laughter, he kissed his wise spouse, took courage, banished his sorrow, and joy again reigned in the house.

The message is clear. Encourage your mate. It will strengthen the marriage *and* quite possibly the bank account as the evidence in chapter 1 indicates.

WHO NEEDS ENCOURAGEMENT?

Everyone needs encouragement, whether it's in the arena of sports, business, or life. Encouragement is often the difference between winning and losing. For example, athletic teams realize the home court or home field gives competing teams a definite advantage. Coaches and players repeatedly say the support of the local fans pulling for them and cheering them on is an advantage worth several points to the home team. The cheerleaders and the crowd may not know the difference between a first down and a touchdown, but they know when their guys do something good, and they let them know. And they often make their support known very vocally. That's the way it should be, could be, oughta be in *your* marriage and mine. Whether the chips are up or down, get on your mate's side and be that cheerleader-encourager.

A wise person observed that when we deserve love the least, we need it the most. The same can be said about encouragement because generally speaking, when we are discouraged, our actions (pity parties, withdrawn attitude, sarcastic comments, angry reactions, etc.) do not motivate our mates to encourage us. *That's* when our love meets the test. That's when the "for better or worse" part of the wedding ceremony takes on real significance. That's when you start making those mammoth deposits in your marriage that are the pure "gold" you can cash in with real delight in your golden years.

Yes, the man is the head of the wife, but that works only if Christ is the head of the man. The thing we all need to remember is that a wife truly wants someone she can look up to, but not someone who will look down on her. Any head of an organization who does not utilize the skills, talent, and intelligence of his executive vice president is simply missing out on a tremendous opportunity to be infinitely more effective as the team leader.

Some people have concrete for a brain: Concrete as in "all mixed up and permanently set."

Furthermore, any man who doesn't consult his wife for her perspective and opinion has a bad case of tunnel vision and concrete for a brain (concrete as in "all mixed up and permanently set"). In business, any CEO worth his salt will always consult carefully and thoroughly with the associates on the team he has put together.

Teams always function better when they're pulling together. The huge Belgian horse is a beautiful example. This powerful animal can pull 8,000 pounds of weight when he's harnessed, but if you put another of those magnificent animals with him, the two can pull 18,000 pounds. Spend a week training them so that they pull in perfect harmony, and the team can pull over 25,000 pounds.

Husbands and wives who are pulling in harmony not only will have more fun in the process but, as a team, can accomplish considerably more than they could as individuals acting on their own.

WANTED: A LEADER_____

Christian psychologist Charles Lowery says one primary reason he counsels Christian couples is the man's failure to assume the spiritual leadership in the family. However, even if the couples have no faith of any kind, I'd like to stress that the principle of having someone in the leadership position is still important!

LEADERSHIP—NOT DICTATORSHIP_____

Here are some paraphrases from *Man of Steel and Velvet* by Aubrey P. Andelin:

> The leadership position is one of trust, for which man is accountable to God. He must accept it, not reject it. He can't give it to someone else. It has been assigned to him.

> Leadership demands firmness, courage, decisive judgment, and fairness, generously blended with tenderness, kindness, consideration, generosity, and humility.

> A man who would fill the leadership role must be a man of convictions and he must stand on those convictions, even when they're not popular.

> Humility is prerequisite to leadership. Once a leader makes a mistake, this enables him to immediately acknowledge the mistake, ask for forgiveness, and then move ahead. No leader, regardless of how great he might be, is infallible.

Leadership involves tenderness and consideration. The man who is unwilling to listen is sowing the seeds of discord, discontent, resentment, and eventually rebellion. A leader listens empathetically to his wife and children because he understands that they want to be heard even when their suggestions are not accepted. The fact that they are heard softens any disappointment they might feel.

A man must lead with consideration, mercy, love, and unselfishness if he is to truly lead his family. The key is unselfishness.

THE SERVANT'S HEART

When you clearly understand and practice these principles of leadership, with all the benefits that come your way, you will abandon forever any authoritarian or dictatorship thoughts or practices and concentrate on filling your leadership position. John Flovio says it well, "Who hath not served cannot command."

> **"Who hath not served
> cannot command."
> —John Flovio**

9 | DON'T BE STUPID

> Although trust in a partner means different things to different people—dependability, loyalty, honesty, fidelity—its essence is emotional safety. While feelings of love or sexual excitement may wax and wane over time, ideally, trust is a constant. When you have trust, you have it all.
>
> —Caryl S. Avery

A wealthy couple decided to employ a chauffeur. The lady of the house advertised, the applicants were screened, and four suitable candidates were brought before her for the final selection. She called the prospective chauffeurs to her balcony and pointed to a brick wall along the driveway. Then she asked the men, "How close do you think you could come to that wall without scratching our limousine?"

The first man felt he could drive within a foot of the wall without damaging the car. The second was confident he could come within six inches. The third believed he could get within three inches.

The fourth candidate told the lady, "I don't really know how close I could come to the wall without damaging your car. I would consider it my responsibility to stay as far away from that wall or any other dangerous area as I could." The fourth candidate got the job because he understood the true skill in driving is based not on the ability to steer the car close to danger but on the ability to maintain a wide margin of safety. Playing it safe is generally the wisest course of action where danger is involved—especially in marriage.

I really do believe a man or a woman who jeopardizes marriage, family, friendships, career, and job by playing with sexual fire is, at the least, *acting* stupidly. Apparently

I'm not alone in this thinking because every time I do the courtship seminar, many husbands and wives who are present enthusiastically nod their approval on this point and many of them verbalize their feelings when the seminar is over.

Although "Don't Be Stupid" may not be the most gracious way to get your attention, the odds are that when you saw the title of this chapter, you immediately dug into the words you've been reading. I could have tried to get your attention more gently, of course, but the subject is so critically important to courtship after marriage that I wanted to make absolutely certain I had your undivided attention.

IS "ROMEO" HAPPY?

Many years ago I briefly worked with a man who truly was the Romeo of the world. I've heard of guys who had a girlfriend in every town; this guy had one on every corner! Interestingly enough, he wasn't particularly good looking, though he wasn't bad looking. He had the ability to make anyone feel at ease around him. He made you, whether you were male or female, feel important. You got the impression that you were the only one around, and this ability endeared him to whomever he was with. This was particularly true of women, so he used his "charm" to seduce large numbers of them. Needless to say, he did not survive long with the company I was with, and for many years we lost contact.

Late one evening as I was returning to my home in Columbia, South Carolina, from an out of town trip, I stopped to get a cup of coffee. When I walked into the little restaurant, I heard his voice: "Zig, over here!" And there sat Romeo. Grinning broadly he approached me, and I asked, "Well, Partner, how're you doing?" He unexpectedly said, "What you really want to know is, 'How is my love life?' " In reality, that was not what was on my mind, but when he said that, I responded, "Well, no, that wasn't what I was asking, but now that you've brought it up, how is your love life?" He smiled broadly and said, "Zig, I met this lonely little housewife who lives at the north end of town, and she was married to an absolute heel! A jerk from the word 'go,' a sorry, low-down, no-good rascal of the first order. So I moved in and took over, and in my lifetime I have never known such joy and excitement. Man, life is absolutely magnificent!"

I obviously looked shocked as I asked, "Well, do I know this lady?" He smiled, and he said, "Sure, you've met my wife." And I said, "Yes, I've met your wife, but explain yourself." With a serious expression on his face, he said, "Well, Zig, I discovered that if I was pleasant to my wife, said many complimentary things to her, gave her my undivided attention, did nice things for her, and was as thoughtful and considerate and kind to her as I had been to all those other women, I had the most beautiful, loving, thoughtful, kind, considerate, romantic human being on the face of this earth under my own roof. How I regret that I did not realize that many years ago." With an even broader grin he said, "But, man, I'm making up for lost time now!" He learned not to act stupid! You and I can learn the same thing from *his* experience.

He sought pleasure—it nearly cost him his happiness. I'm convinced that there are thousands, maybe even millions, of husbands and wives who've had similar experiences.

SEX CAN "WARM" YOU OR "BURN" YOU

One of the real delights in my life is to sit in front of a good, warm fire in a fireplace on a cold, crisp winter evening or a damp dreary day. Few things are as enjoyable as curling up with a good book next to a fire or sitting there with The Redhead holding hands and watching the embers crackle and pop.

In may ways, sex is like fire, except it's far more exciting. Sex in marriage, where *it* belongs, and fire in a fireplace, where *it* belongs, are warm, delightful, and absolute pleasures. But if fire spreads beyond the hearth for which it is designed, or sex spreads beyond the marriage bed, it burns us and becomes incredibly destructive.

Building a magnificent relationship is difficult, if not impossible, without the proper perspective on sex. The evidence is conclusive that any sexual relationship outside marriage will "burn" us and cause our lives and marriages to go up in smoke as well.

A RADICAL APPROACH

Several years ago a reporter from a Texas magazine was interviewing me, and he asked me if I, from time to time, took my secretary to lunch. I responded, "Of course not!" He was somewhat stunned at my reply and asked the obvious question, "What do you mean, 'Of course not!'?" I responded that there were several reasons for the answer. First, I pointed out that my secretary and I have absolutely nothing to discuss at lunch that we could not discuss more advantageously in my office with the door wide open. Next, I explained that my secretary, who is now my administrative assistant, is an extraordinarily bright lady and would not go to lunch with me.

Third, I reminded him that some people were inclined to be critical of such conduct and I felt that my example must be such that I would not knowingly subject myself to that kind of criticism.

I also pointed out that The Redhead agreed with my

first three reasons. Then there is the obvious reality that if I took my secretary to lunch once, I might want to take her again, and the only thing that kind of relationship could lead to was trouble, spelled with a capital "T." I elaborated by saying that 50 percent of all divorces are caused by a man or a woman meeting a member of the opposite sex in the marketplace and becoming attracted to that person. In 70 percent of these cases, the man and the woman were working either in the same department or in close proximity to each other. In short, I had everything to lose and nothing to gain from a "business" lunch with my secretary.

The bottom line or, as my friend and associate Jim Savage would say, the "Reader's Digest" is this: The real reason I won't take any lady, other than my wife, to lunch is that I love my wife far too much to give her one moment of discomfort or take even the most remote chance of damaging our relationship over any "friendship" I might have with any woman, anywhere.

"JUST" FRIENDS

Now, I'm absolutely convinced that most people kid themselves when they say, "This member of the opposite sex and I are 'just' friends." That might well be true in some cases, and it might well be true in the beginning of many relationships. But in far, far, FAR TOO MANY cases, this "friendship" with the opposite sex, *over a period of time* because of the mutual respect for the intellect or professional capabilities of the other, changes into something more than friendship. Gradually, your relationship becomes more "open" and trusting. You start sharing little bits of privileged information, and the conversation gets more intimate as you notice the "coincidences" that happen and the "similarities" you share. This tends to highlight the "differences" between you and your mate, and it appears that you and your new-found interest agree on "everything" while you and your mate agree on nothing. Then because of the strong "compatibility" factor or physical attractiveness of the other person, those hormones are activated, and in all too many cases the inevitable happens: The "love," which you never intended to happen, "just happened."

Denial is not a river in Egypt; denial is ignoring the obvious.

Tragically, most attractions are denied in the beginning with catastrophic results. The meeting of the eyes for a tenth of a second too long; the passing of each other in a corridor and giving a "special" acknowledgment; the "accidental" bumping into each other in the parking lot or the coffee shop; the one-second extended touching of hands with the exchange of a greeting or the passing of paper from one to the other—these and many more "clues" are "red flags" that must not be ignored. Denial is not a river in Egypt! Denial is ignoring the obvious. Most people who have enough sense to get out of a telephone booth without written instructions on the side are aware when two people are attracted to each other. When this happens, rather than pretend that it didn't happen, why not: (a) honestly acknowledge what has happened; (b) remember your commitment to your mate; and (c) remind yourself of the proven fact that there are no "harmless" flirtations?

CREATIVE FIDELITY_____

Instead of using the "it's no big thing" excuse, have the courage to take the moral responsibility at the precise moment you recognize the danger. Put the brakes on, back away, and carefully avoid any unnecessary activity that could be misleading. It's important to put the brakes on early because according to Dr. Willard F. Harley, Jr., a licensed clinical psychologist, "Affairs usually develop insidiously, often in long term working relationships between people of the opposite sex, and often because we misunderstand the concept of commitment." As Harley explains, "It's not a simple matter of me saying to my wife, 'I commit myself to you, Joyce,' but rather 'I will do my best to take care of you and to meet your needs.'" The goal of your commitment in marriage should be that your spouse would never want to have an affair.

Jane Ellens takes this concept a step further with what she describes as "creative fidelity." She states, "Fidelity within marriage is far more than just putting a leash on lust. Faithfulness involves affirmative action, not just refraining from extramarital sex. It requires faithfulness to the vows we have made, vows to be constantly 'person-centered' in our marriage, to consider always the well-being of the other, and to practice honest, open communication." She terms creative fidelity a "dedication to the freedom, maturity and growth of one's spouse."

NO TRUST—NO HAPPINESS

The importance of trust in a marriage was underscored in a column written by Steven Covey in the January 1988 edition of *Executive Excellence*. Covey was conducting a seminar at a beautiful site on the Oregon coast when he was approached by a man who asked for a private audience.

The man began the conversation by saying, "Look at this wonderful coastline. I should be having a great time—yet I really don't enjoy coming to these seminars."

The man had Covey's attention. When asked why, he

replied, "All I can think about is the grilling I'm going to get from my wife on the phone tonight. She gives me the third degree every time I'm away from home. 'Who did I have breakfast with? What did we talk about? What did I do for entertainment? Who was with me?'"

The man added, "And the tone of her interrogation is always, 'Who can I call to confirm all this?'"

Covey continued interacting with the man who finally offered an interesting observation. "I guess she knows all the questions to ask," he sheepishly said, "because it was on a trip like this that I met her . . . when I was married to some-one else."

Considering the implications of his statement, Covey responded, "You're really into quick fix, aren't you?"

"What do you mean?" the man replied.

Covey's comment was, "My friend, you can't *talk* your-self out of a problem you *behave* yourself into."

At that point Covey proceeded to share what I believe was some really on-target counsel, "The best way to change her attitude and win her trust is to open an emotional bank account with her and start making deposits, and don't expect quick results. You'll need to make a thousand and one deposits in that account over time before you see a significant change."

Covey went on to explain that deposits are made through courtesy and kindness, as well as through honesty and commitment. Withdrawals from these emotional accounts are made through discourtesy, disrespect, threats, and overreaction. Both the trust factor and the comfort factor in a relationship, I believe, are built through the kind, courteous, and honest deposits that say, "You can trust me because I'm trustworthy." Chances are excellent, however, that complete trust will be a long time coming; this wife clearly knows how he relates to and deals with "other" women because at one time she was the "other" woman. Makes you wonder what the man's "happiness" situation would be if he had courted his first wife as enthusiastically and loyally as he did this second one, doesn't it? Easily, the cruelest cut of all in the marital relationship is when one partner cuts the cord of trust with the act of adultery.

FAITHFULNESS AND HAPPINESS

Just how important is this matter of trust and faithfulness? For many years now, I've crisscrossed the country beating the bushes, conducting personal growth and educational seminars. During that time, I've enjoyed pleasures, privileges, and contacts that few people have had the opportunity to enjoy. I've spoken on the platform with two presidents of the United States as well as senators, congressmen, governors, and the secretary of defense. I'm able to count as friends a couple of men who are worth over $1 billion each. I've rubbed elbows with athletic superstars, entertainment giants, and ordinary people.

> **I have never known a person who was married *and* happy who was not 100 percent faithful to his or her mate.**

For fourteen years, as a salesperson, I was in homes where I could literally look through the floor and see the ground underneath, or look up and see the stars through the roof. I have crossed every socioeconomic, racial, ethnic, or religious line our country has to offer.

During that time, through all those experiences, I never met a single human being who was married, and who was happy, who was not *100 percent faithful to his or her mate*. Period!

Now, I'm not preaching or even moralizing. I'm just explaining that if you want to be happy and you're married, you have no options or choices. You must be absolutely loyal. Period. End of statement. Paul Johnson, writing in the *United Reporter*, explains it this way, "The truth is the only sensible advice . . . and can be summed up in six words: *Chastity before marriage, fidelity within it.*" Your question: If what you say is true, why do so many men and women get involved in extramarital affairs? My answer: Most of them are "confused." Read on.

PLEASURE SEEKING—OR—HAPPINESS ACHIEVING

In order to build a lifetime marriage that produces contentment as well as happiness, we need to understand the basic difference between pleasure and happiness. This understanding is critically important because in our pleasure-centered world today, we have almost made pleasure our god, the all-in-all, and the end result.

What's the difference between pleasure and happiness? Well, pleasure is very temporary whereas happiness is of much longer duration. Pleasure is an act we indulge in; happiness is a state of being. The dictionary says that *pleasure* is "gratification, delight, enjoyment, joy." With pleasure, enjoyment dissipates and is frivolous. What we wish for, desire, or "will" that often manifests itself in sensual gratification is called pleasure.

The dictionary says that *happiness* is "a state of well-being, a graceful attitude, good luck, prosperity." Synonyms

> **"B**efore indulging in pleasure, ask three questions: (1) Can I repeat this pleasure indefinitely and be happy? (2) Would I be willing for my mate to know that I have indulged in this pleasure? (3) Will this pleasure be at the expense of someone else's happiness?"
> —Zig Ziglar

for *happiness* are *felicity, beatitude, blessedness,* and *bliss*. Happiness applies to the enjoyment or satisfaction that goes with our well-being. A deeply refined enjoyment that rises from the purest affections is called happiness.

In short, happiness is a much deeper and longer lasting feeling. However, I'd like to emphasize that there are many pleasures in life that all of us enjoy enormously, and I am no exception to the rule. As a matter of fact, I'm convinced that no one will truly find happiness unless there is some pleasure involved along the way.

Before we indulge in any pleasure, we should ask ourselves three very important questions:

1. Can I repeat this pleasure indefinitely and be happy? First example: I love sweets; I could eat a dessert three times a day, 7 days a week, 365 days a year, and snack on something sweet between meals. Eating the sweets would really give me considerable pleasure. The question is, how happy would I be at 486 pounds? Second example: I've been repeatedly told that crack cocaine gives incredible pleasure, but I can assure you, scientifically speaking, that repeated uses of cocaine or crack cocaine will destroy the brain's capacity to reproduce dopamine and norepinephrine. Without these two natural chemicals in your system, it is impossible to experience joy, pleasure, and happiness. The irony is that people ingest the coke to be happy and it destroys any possibility of their being happy. So back to the original question: Can I repeat this pleasure indefinitely and be happy? If the answer is "no," I encourage you to approach the quest for pleasure with extreme caution.

2. *Would I be willing for my mate to know that I have indulged in this pleasure?* A sexual relationship outside matrimony yields a "no" answer (and a "no" answer will preserve many marriages). Even the beginnings of an "overly friendly" relationship that leads to adultery can be headed off with this question: Would I be willing for my mate to know I took an extra forty-five minutes at lunch with a co-worker (of the opposite sex) to counsel him or her on "personal" problems? Would I be willing for my mate to know I took off work at noon today so "the gang" and I could go to our favorite "watering hole" for a few laughs and a few "cold ones"? Getting in the habit of asking this question BEFORE THE ACTION will save much heartache and grief "after the fact."

3. *Will this pleasure be at the expense of someone else's happiness?* If the answer is "yes," you simply refrain from that pleasure. Spending all free time with "buddies" or golfing (hunting, fishing, working) might bring some pleasure, but what about the family's happiness? I had an associate once who passed up the chance for two fifty-yard-line tickets for a Dallas Cowboys vs. Washington Redskins football game to see his child perform in a church play. The pleasure he would have gotten from attending that ball game dimmed considerably in comparison to the happiness in that child's eyes when the son knew just how important he was to his dad.

If I were to take 99 percent of the profit from our company for my personal bank account, I could be involved in some pleasurable activities. However, the growth of our company and our ability to spread the message would be limited. Our ability to compensate the eighty-plus employees of the Zig Ziglar Corporation would be limited, and this not only would be unfair but would make them unhappy. It is absolutely impossible to build happiness on the misery of someone else.

IS ADULTERY *THAT* BAD?

If you think I overstate the seriousness of adultery and the importance of fidelity to your mate, I urge you to look carefully at the results of a *USA Today* survey of three thousand women and one thousand men. The study revealed that seven out of ten men *and* women felt fidelity is more important than a good sexual relationship. When asked which was more important—fidelity or financial security—six out of ten women and five out of ten of the men chose fidelity. Almost half of the men and women agreed that fidelity is even more important than their children. And the overwhelming majority (75 percent) of the women and men agreed with the observation that fidelity is more important than keeping romance alive. The conclusion is inescapable: *Faithfulness* to each other makes all the other romantic parts of marriage much more exciting and gives the marriage the stability that is prerequisite for growth and happiness.

Thought: Would it "turn you on" sexually if you thought your mate was thinking about the most recent episode with a "lover" while the two of you were making love?

With this in mind, I strongly encourage you to pick an appropriate time when you and your mate are not rushed for time and openly discuss this subject. Candidly ask your spouse *after* reading this chapter whether he or she agrees or disagrees with what I'm saying. The odds are astronomical that if your mate *really loves you*, he or she will agree that it makes good sense not to play games where everyone stands a much greater chance of losing than winning. Countless wives in our public seminars have already confirmed this. One heartbroken wife, who seemed to be everything a man could want in a wife, tearfully told me how she had expressed her concerns when her husband took his new secretary to lunch. Her husband told her that she was being jealous and unreasonable, accused her of not "trusting" him, and encouraged her not to worry about a thing. A year later one more marriage had bitten the dust, and three kids under eight no longer had a daddy at home.

BASICALLY SPEAKING

The basic problem, as I've indicated, is that when we cross the line from friendliness to flirtation, an affair could well result. Then one of three things happens—and they are all bad. The affair destroys your marriage and perhaps the marriage of your partner. The affair leads to your mate's distrust of you, and without trust there can be no happiness or peace of mind in the marriage. The affair could lead to another and yet another and in this day of AIDS that could be fatal. More than one affair you think you "get by with" could lead to promiscuity that destroys your capacity to make lasting commitments to anyone or anything. Promiscuous people simply can't trust, and trust is an essential component for lasting relationships. Genuine happiness comes from relationships—not things—and in immoral sexual relationships, people are generally viewed as things, objects for pleasure.

PERSONALLY I DON'T TRUST ME _____

One young woman, who heard me say in a speech that I would never take another woman to dinner, wrote me and said that I must not trust myself and that my faith must not be very strong. I responded that she was right on at least one of those—I do not trust me, meaning my nature, nor do I grow arrogant in my faith that God will not permit me to be tempted beyond what I can bear. I fervently believe He's right, but I also know I can, by choice, get into situations that permit no reasonable chance for escape. I'm simply unwilling to do that.

That's one of the reasons why, when I speak in other cities, I make every effort to avoid being picked up by a lady alone. Even on book tours, which I regularly do, when I am to be escorted by members of the media or the public relations firms, I avoid being escorted by one lady. Some might say that's going to a ridiculous extreme; they could be right, but the possibility that they are wrong tells me I am doing what is best for me.

For what it's worth, let me repeat that The Redhead approves of my procedures along those lines 100 percent. I might even add that she *enthusiastically* approves of my approach. As my mother said to me so many times when I was growing up, "It's better to be safe than to be sorry." The fact is, I have very little to gain by tempting fate, and I have an enormous amount to lose. I don't take a simple bet of a dollar on the golf course or anywhere else; I'm simply not a gambler. I certainly would not, therefore, gamble on negatively affecting or destroying my relationship with the one who means everything to me for the "questionable" at best, "dangerous" at worst, pleasure of spending time with a member of the opposite sex.

TEMPTATION—AND DISASTER—CAN COME AT ANY TIME

A former colleague lost his wife of thirty-nine years when she became involved in a casual "have a cup of coffee relationship," which developed into an affair, which led to divorce and marriage to this man who was "just a friend, my goodness, he's much younger than I am." Later, that marriage, too, ended in separation. Yet another associate, after over fifty years of matrimony that included children, grandchildren, and great-grandchildren, took up with a younger woman and divorced his wife.

I do not know all the factors involved in these divorces, but there are two things I do know. First of all, trust was broken, adultery was committed, and families were devastated all the way to the third generation—so far. Second, both divorces would have been avoided had commonsense principles been followed.

WILL VS. IMAGINATION

The best way to protect your body from adulterous actions is to protect your mind from lustful and adulterous thoughts. The reason is obvious. Adultery is always committed in the mind before it is committed physically. When you feed your mind with pornographic magazines, suggestive videos and TV programs, soap operas, and R-rated movies, you are feeding your imagination with powerful suggestions that eventually will weaken your moral resolve when you are confronted with sexual temptation. A wise man has observed, "When will meets imagination, bet your money on imagination." Avoid this "garbage" being input in your mind. It is true that "as ye sow so also shall ye reap."

Norman Cousins said it very well in the *Saturday Review:*

> The trouble with this wide open pornography . . . is not that it corrupts, but that it *desensitizes;* not that it unleashes the passions, but that it cripples the emotions; not that it encourages a mature attitude, but that it is a reversion to infantile obsessions; not that it removes the blinders, but that it distorts the view. Prowess is proclaimed, but love is denied. What we have is not liberation, but dehumanization.

When a man views pornography, his wife can become less and less attractive to him. He starts comparing seventeen- and eighteen-year-old models with his wife of many years who has borne two or three children. That's unrealistic and absolutely disastrous. Pornography derives its drive from lust. Lust is not the result of an overactive sex drive. According to Richard Exley, lust is not a biological phenomenon or the by-product of our glands. If it were, lust could be satisfied with the sexual experience, like a glass of water quenches thirst or a good meal satisfies appetite. But Exley observes that the more we attempt to appease our lust, the more demanding it becomes.

Exley points out that when we deny our lustful obsessions, we are not repressing a legitimate drive; we are putting to death an aberration. He compares the relationship between lust and the gift of sex to that between a cancerous cell and a normal cell. He then recommends that denying it doesn't make us "sexless saints," but frees us to fully and uninhibitedly express ourselves sexually within the context of marriage. I'm recommending the same approach to pornography Nancy Reagan used in her war on drugs, "Just Say No."

FIND A MENTOR

Another practical step—and one being advocated much more frequently these days—is to share your struggles and weaknesses with someone with whom you can be accountable, either your spouse or a friend of the same sex. If prominent spiritual and political leaders who experienced moral failures had taken this precaution, many of them would not have seen their careers shattered or their ministries devastated and their personal lives broken.

Earlier I said that you should not share marital problems with friends. I am not being contradictory here. The key issue is accountability. If you are struggling with an issue that you have recognized as a danger, share your concern with a person specially qualified to "mentor" you. One pastor I know established a group of three other men who met on a regular basis to discuss ethical issues and personal "weaknesses." They worked to hold each other accountable. If a situation ever came up where there was a concern about the proper response, these men were only a "helping" phone call away. They also agreed to share any moral/ethical "failures" that had occurred since their last meeting. Knowing they were going to be accountable to family *and* friends helped each one enormously.

FAMILY FIRST

Another important step is to avoid emotional entanglements or dependencies. Helping others at the expense of the well-being of your own marriage and family is never God's will, and certainly not trying to help a member of the opposite sex when it might harm your own spouse. Frequently, such emotional entanglements, though well-intentioned, lead directly to sexual involvement. I saw this happen to a young minister friend of mine with two young children as he counseled, comforted, and helped a young divorcee get over the pain of her husband leaving her for another woman. The sad thing, too, is the fact that this is another case where the minister's wife immediately sensed the danger and pleaded with her husband to back off. He thought she was being silly, but his family became another divorce statistic.

Guard your work relationships with members of the opposite sex. It is essential to keep them on a professional basis. Limits on both time and the level of friendship need to be monitored. It's always important to make sure that your wife is on a deeper level of friendship with you than your business associates or that your friends or business acquaintances of the opposite sex do not look to you to meet their emotional needs.

"There are several good protections against temptations, but the surest is cowardice."
—Mark Twain

Mark Twain gave us good advice when he wrote, "There are several good protections against temptation, but the surest is cowardice." Mark Twain wasn't a theologian, but he was scripturally accurate with that advice because the Bible clearly tells us to flee from youthful lusts.

MEN, PROTECT YOUR WIVES _____

One of the tragedies of our free and open society is that all too often husbands and wives form friendships with other apparently "nice" couples in a close-knit group. Over a period of time they grow close, comfortable, and even intimate in their relationship. As a result, many of the barriers of common sense and decency are broken down. Too many times there is a relaxing of moral standards, and the group might turn to watching questionable videos or even downright pornographic movies. All too often they start telling those funny, slightly dirty, suggestive stories that generate a certain amount of laughter but a considerably larger amount of broken down inhibitions.

Gentlemen, I can tell you that when that happens, you have a strong obligation and responsibility to protest as strongly as is necessary to put a stop to it. You need to protect your wife from that kind of exposure. Here's why. Though things might have (I did say *might* have) started out "innocently" enough, familiarity does breed "attempt." Exposure to immoral talk and actions leads to immoral thought, which *always* precedes immoral actions.

Many times, even in a small group, there will be a man or a woman who is literally "prospecting" for an affair. The individual closely watches and listens to the responses of an intended victim (and victim is what he or she is, albeit many times a willing one!). When the "prospect" responds enthusiastically to the suggestions or vulgarity, the "predator" takes notice, and the seduction process is set in motion. Later, a casual drop-by or a chance meeting in the grocery store is followed by a phone call ostensibly to talk to the mate; and over a period of time an affair develops.

One of the most tragic events of life is to see a man or woman lose his or her mate and "best friend" at the same time. Some of you who read this might protest that you would never make friends with a person of that character. If you really believe that, my friend, you're living in a dream world, and I fervently hope and pray for your sake that it never happens.

The reality is that a person who has passions aroused and inhibitions released through coarse language or pornographic viewing and often fed with alcohol or other drugs will not let moral inhibitions or "character" stop the imagination dead in its tracks. The best time to put a stop to questionable activity is the first time it raises its head. It's not a question of being a "goody-two-shoes"; it's a question of being prudent and protective of your mate, your marriage and, yes, yourself.

A UNIVERSAL LAW

You are what you are and where you are because of what's gone into your mind; you can change what you are and where you are by changing what goes into your mind. What you feed your mind influences your thinking. Your thinking, of course, controls your actions. Adultery is never an instant action. It is conceived in the mind, and the input into the mind certainly has an impact on your thinking and actions. If you don't believe me, ask Jimmy Swaggart. I say that not as a put-down of Swaggart, nor do I say it lightly. His fall was one of the tragedies of Christendom. Our prayer truly is that God will restore him, but in the meantime, millions of lives have been negatively influenced because he got involved in pornography, which influenced his thinking, which influenced his actions.

Study after study reveals that the husband who watches pornographic presentations on film or looks at *Playboy*, *Penthouse*, or other magazines of that caliber will, over a period of time, find his wife less and less attractive. The husband whose imagination runs wild while staring at an eighteen-year-old nude in *Playboy* will have his mind focused on her, and even as he is romancing his own wife, his thoughts may be on the picture in *Playboy*. Adultery, according to the Bible, has just been committed. Many times it's just a question of time before the mental act of adultery will be physically consummated.

IMAGINATION VS. REALITY

Though men are more sight oriented than women, I hasten to add that the wife who watches the daily soaps is courting real trouble. On a regular basis she sees unrealistic—even grossly distorted—dramatizations of love, sex, infidelity, abortions, and affairs. Once a woman gets into the habit of watching these "beautiful people," she begins to instinctively or subconsciously compare them to the rather "drab" person she's married to. All her own mate does is work hard, remain faithful, provide loving companionship, help create a home, and generally add to her health, wealth, and happiness. Sounds pretty boring when she compares him to that nonexistent product of the creative mind of a highly paid writer who does nothing but dream up those "hunks" on TV.

The reality is that a person's imagination has the capacity to run absolutely wild, and once the imagination goes to work, you can rest assured that the reality of a mate who has been loving and faithful for twenty years cannot compare to the dashing young doctor or attorney who is so loving, brilliant, compassionate, thoughtful, considerate, and attentive to his companion with whom he has a "meaningful relationship" there on TV. In a nutshell, ladies, I encourage you, especially if you are at home each day, to leave those "soaps" alone—they can have a damaging impact on your relationship with your mate.

Question: Do you honestly believe you can regularly watch the "soaps" and be both optimistic and morally sound?

Why take chances? The best way to court your mate physically is to court your mate mentally. As Solomon said, "Think back on the days of your youth." In the videotape of your mind, remember how enormously attractive and appealing your mate was to you when you first met. That's the tape you need to play in your mind. Let your imagination run wild. You surely remember the anticipation you had prior to the consecration of your marriage. For days, weeks, or even months and years, you imagined the total joy that would be yours when you claimed your mate on your wedding day. *That's* the tape you should replay in your mind. It will enhance your relationship with your mate, and you will be bonded closer and closer together. As a matter of fact, the literal command that you are to "cleave" together means that you will become "one flesh," which will make it impossible for another man or woman to come between you.

ONE LAST THOUGHT

I conclude this chapter with the simplest, shortest, neatest, most practical, and effective bit of advice to keep you from the tragedy of adultery and divorce I've ever heard. My good friend Dr. James Merritt from Snellville, Georgia, shared this with me. Every night he and his wife, Theresa, as they bid each other good night with their statements that they love each other, conclude the statement with, "And I just want you to know that I was faithful to you today." Wow!

From the day we heard this, my wife and I have done the same thing every night. Husbands and wives, I'm absolutely convinced that if you will immediately start doing the same thing, whether you've been married two days or sixty years, it will strengthen your marriage and dramatically reduce the possibility that either of you will go astray.

Think about it. If you knew you were going to confront that issue *every* night before you went to sleep, don't you believe you would act accordingly? Accountability is a powerful deterrent.

10 | WHEN YOU FIGHT— FIGHT FAIR

Only the brave know how to forgive. A coward
never forgives. It is not in his nature.
—Robert Muller

A man and a woman experienced their very first quarrel during the fiftieth year of their wedded life. The man tucked a gracious note under his wife's pillow that read: "My darling bride, let's put off quarreling until after the honeymoon is over. Signed: Your devoted husband." That's the ideal way to fight, but realistically, most of us would not have the grace, love, patience, or temperament to pull that one off. On the other hand, we can surely do better than the next example.

Some years ago a story appeared on the wires of United Press International. A young New York bride got into an argument with her husband of just a few hours, ran him down with a car, and killed him on the way home from the wedding reception.

The county district attorney said the twenty-one-year-old bride drove over her twenty-three-year-old husband after the couple argued violently on their way from the cocktail lounge where the reception was held.

This will come as no shock to you, but allow me to state the obvious: Every couple will experience *some* conflict. After all, as marriage expert H. Norman Wright points out, "Couples who have developed harmony are *not* those who are identical in thinking behavior and attitudes—they are not carbon copies of each other. They are the couples who have learned to take their differences through the process of

191

acceptance, understanding and eventually complimentation. Differing from another person is very natural and normal and adds an edge of excitement to a relationship." According to Wright and other marriage counselors, conflict is a natural phenomenon, since everyone's values and needs differ. Furthermore, conflict provides an opportunity for growth in a relationship. I guess you might say conflict is a little like dynamite. Properly handled it can be helpful. But if used at the wrong time or in the wrong manner, it can be terribly destructive.

SELFISH INDEPENDENCE

The question that begs an answer is, why would there be conflict between two people who love each other anyhow? The answer lies in human nature, which is basically selfish. Acting alone, selfishly, is basic to every marriage problem, the essence of sin, the worm in every apple. It is wanting "my own way," with money, time, decisions, sex; thinking of personal comfort, pleasure, rights; insisting on independence and personal ambitions at my partner's expense; ignoring my partner's feelings and desires (spoken or unspoken); living in my own small circle, my private world; refusing to go the second mile to serve, give, please, adapt, submit; concerning myself more with a personal victory than a stronger relationship. To eliminate this selfishness, we must always ask this key question: "Am I being selfish and independent in this matter right now?" Love, real love, doesn't *demand*; it *serves*.

If you have been a serious reader up to now, you know that I have spoken more to the husbands than to the wives. I do this for two reasons. First, more men than women are guilty of being less sensitive to the needs of their mate. Second, men have the greater responsibility because of the unique position they occupy in the chain of command, so let's look at some of the problems in the marriage relationship.

MEN ARE SPOILED

Our society, and, yes, that includes our mothers, helped considerably in the "spoiling" of the typical male. Just notice and you'll see the signs everywhere. A typical family sits down to watch TV, and if there's a "game" (football, baseball, basketball, etc.) on, Dad or husband "expects" to watch it; and without conferring with anyone, he just turns the television to "his" channel.

He's had a tough week (Mom had nothing to do), so he gets up on Saturday morning and heads for the golf course or his favorite fishing hole. After all, he "deserves" some relaxation. He comes in after a hard day's work, plops down on the sofa, and "orders" (pleasantly and with a smile, of course) a cup of coffee or glass of tea while he watches the news and collects his thoughts.

He gets up early for his jog or walk because he's got to stay in shape, and the wife can easily get the kids up, dress them, prepare breakfast, get dressed, and be ready to eat with him when he's shaved and showered after the run.

He buys the new shotgun, though the budget is tight, because all of his life he's wanted one, and if he waits until everything is "paid up" and all the circumstances are "just right," he might be too old to enjoy it. He gets up from the dinner table and turns on the TV because he's looked forward all week to "his" program. Besides, it won't take that long for his wife to wash the dishes, clean the kitchen, and put the kids to bed. Then they can watch the news together because "quality" time is important. Then the exhausted wife (the husband can't understand why) and the well-fed, relaxed, and rested husband head for bed. Interestingly enough, he's surprised, hurt, puzzled, disappointed, frustrated, and possibly even angry that she's not just as interested in fun and games as he is. After all, he is married to that woman, and his father or grandfather made it clear to him that "sex" was his "right."

O.K., I'll admit that many husbands are not quite that far gone, but too many of us were raised to "expect" to receive a lot more than we deliver. In addition, most of us fellows have too much "little boy" in us and not only expect our way, but all too often *demand* our way and pout when we don't get it.

SHAME ON ME

I plead guilty, with embarrassment, to the following incident because it makes an important point:

Just a few months after we got married and settled into a little apartment in Columbia, South Carolina, The Redhead decided to go home for a visit with her folks. At the time, that puzzled me. I remember wondering why any eighteen-year-old girl would want to go see her mama less than a year after she had gotten married. Especially since she had such a good, kind, and loving husband. Can you relate to my thoughts, fellows? Feeling "abused," rejected, and just one step away from martyrdom, I gallantly agreed and gave her my "permission" to make the trip. However, we did set the exact date for her to come back, and I expected her to be there at that *precise* moment.

About two hours before she was to arrive, I received a telephone call. It was The Redhead telling me she had delayed her return for twenty-four hours. Boy, was I ever upset. As I recall, I told her I was expecting her home instead of a telephone call, and I was not only disappointed, but mad, and I wanted her "back home." Then, in a rather immature burst of temper and insecurity, generously blended with selfishness, I hung up the phone. (How much "fun" do you think she had the next twenty-four hours? But I "showed" her.)

Well, The Redhead did arrive the next day, but in my childish and rather petty way, I set about to "punish" her for doing such a dastardly deed. I even went to bed in the other bedroom, despite the fact that she had sincerely apologized for her "unforgivable" action. Eventually, I came to my senses and realized that I was acting in a childish, selfish, and immature manner. I apologized and asked for forgiveness. She granted it, and the case was closed.

Unfortunately, The Redhead was miserable from the moment she made that phone call until I apologized and asked her to forgive me. *However,* she was not nearly as miserable as I was. Message: When you build a wall between each other, misery for both is the inevitable result, and the only way to remove the misery is for the one who built the wall to dismantle it by asking for forgiveness.

SHE DOESN'T EXIST, FELLOWS

In this era of disposable marriages, the myth of the "hyphenated" wife continues to plague us, though she never has existed and never will. There is no energy tank large enough to supply the fuel needed to be a supermom—dedicated employee—committed housekeeper—chauffeur extraordinaire—hostess and entertainer deluxe—homework helper specialist—magnificent meal-maker—confidante—companion—and passionate love-maker. Just to look at *one* of these functions, not counting that last one, is enough to exhaust the average male!

The process of overcommitment, misplaced values, and lack of sensitivity to a mate's needs inevitably lead to conflict that can bring on disillusionment, bitterness, and divorce or a tension-laden marriage. In plain English, fellows, if our mates work as hard outside the home and two or three times as hard inside the home as we do, resentment fueled by fatigue is the inevitable result.

Don't misunderstand. The husband isn't always the "bad guy" by any stretch of the imagination. In my years in direct sales and countless additional experiences since then, I've seen many cases where the husband worked many hours overtime to provide for his family and then came home to a messy house and prepared his own dinner. Or too often the husband, exhausted from a grueling day, was greeted by a sloppy wife who demanded to know why he forgot to pick up the cleaning on his way home. So what's the answer?

BALANCE IS THE KEY

In this busy world of ours, husbands and wives often get so wrapped up with their careers, friends, hobbies, etc., that they neglect their relationships with each other. As Charles Swindoll says, "We worship our work; we work at our play and we play at our worship."

My friend Mary Kay Ash, the founder of Mary Kay Cosmetics, told *U.S. News & World Report*, "I like to work long hours, but if you have to lose your husband or family in the process, you're doing things the wrong way. It's no fun to count your money by yourself." One reason for Mary Kay's enormous success is the fact that in her career she encouraged her people to keep God first, family second, and business third.

That approach is effective because it keeps your life on an even keel and in balance. That's important because any time you "put all your eggs in one basket," if something happens to the basket, you're in trouble. For example, men (and some women) too often stake everything on their career. Then if they lose their job, their company goes under or is bought out, they are devastated because their self-worth was tied up in their job.

Industrial psychologist David Sirota puts it this way: The real problem comes when your self-esteem is based almost entirely on work performance. Sirota points out that a normal, healthy person has three aspects to life—work, play, and love—and to maintain balance in his life, he must give himself to all three.

The husband or wife who is committed only to a career has a spouse who suffers from a low self-image because of being neglected. She—or he—may become depressed or angry, which could lead to withdrawal, drug or alcohol abuse, extramarital affairs, or simply a lifeless relationship. All of these lead to conflict that, if left unresolved, can destroy the marriage.

Tim Kimmel, in his book *Little House on the Freeway*, points out that driven overachievers can also exist outside the workplace, for example, mothers who are caught up in Little League, piano lessons, school activities, or even church activities.

Leading A Balanced Life

1. Place an "X" on each spoke coming from the hub in the center of the configuration ranking where you stand in each area *today:* "1" is poor; "10" is excellent.
2. Connect the "X's" in a circular fashion.
3. Write your first name in the center of the hub of spokes.
4. Write "Wheel of Life" on the blank line above the spoke.

This drawing represents your "Wheel of Life," and if your ride through life is not as smooth as you would like for it to be, the road may not be your problem! While it's true that you could be at all "1's" and be in balance, you wouldn't progress as quickly as you might like.

For an interesting experiment, try the following:

1. Draw a "Wheel of Life" for yourself and your spouse (where you think your spouse would rate himself or herself).

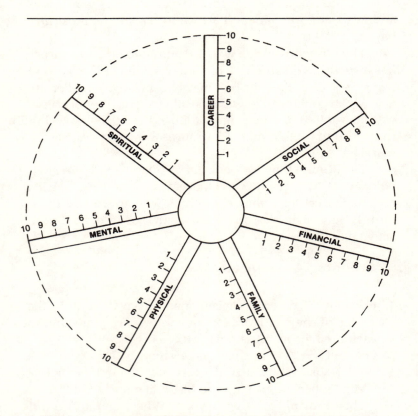

2. Have your spouse do the same thing independently.
3. Get together to discuss and compare graphs.
4. Set mutual goals in areas where you would both like to grow.

Bryan Flanagan, an outstanding speaker/trainer and a friend of mine, shared that while living in San Francisco several years ago, he did the exercise as I have outlined it here.

If your ride through life is not as smooth as you would like for it to be, the road may not be your problem.

He rated himself an "8" on the social spoke while his wife, Cyndi, rated herself a "2." Bryan thought they both were at an "8" because he was out and about every day: riding the BART train into the city with his "buddies," going to lunch with coworkers, visiting clients. His exposure to people was frequent. Cyndi, on the other hand, was at home (by her choice) caring for one-year-old Patrick Flanagan. And as Bryan says, "Cyndi is a great mother and wife and was truly enjoying her days as a full-time mom. As a former teacher, she had looked forward to staying home with our children. However, her view of social life (reading books to a one-year-old, and talking to a few—very few—moms also raising one-year-olds) was limited. The wheel helped us notice the situation and make immediate improvements."

Bryan and Cyndi started a "date night"; once every week (or at least every other week) they would bring in a sitter and go out together. On other weekends, they had friends with small children over to visit. Also, Bryan became extra helpful on weekends, freeing Cyndi to do whatever she wanted with her newly acquired "free time."

My point is simple. By evaluating the situation, Bryan and Cyndi were able to develop a plan that kept them in "balance." You can do the same thing.

BALANCE AND SERENITY

Balance is critical, and so is serenity or contentment. Reinhold Niebuhr wrote, "God, give us grace to accept with serenity the things that cannot be changed, courage to change the things which should be changed, and the wisdom to distinguish the one from the other." If we develop serenity and balance, we'll discover, in our marriage relationship, we have time—time for the little things, even time to court our mates and play with our kids.

The Serenity Prayer: "God, give us grace to accept with serenity the things that cannot be changed, courage to change the things which should be changed, and the wisdom to distinguish one from the other." —Reinhold Neibuhr

---

My friend and colleague, Sheilah Murray Bethel, points out that she has never heard a man say at the end of his career, "If I had it to do over, I'd get up earlier and go down to the corporation and get on with my career. I'd stay later and work harder." She has heard, and so have I, many men say, "If I had it to do over, I'd spend more time with my family. I'd get to know my kids better. I'd court my wife more." The irony of it all, as I clearly spelled out in the first chapter, is that had he invested *more* time in his family, he would have in all likelihood gone further in his career. There would also have been less conflict and fewer "fights" in the marriage.

To improve your chances of never having to utter those "If I had it to do over" words, let's explore how you fight fairly so both of you win. That's important because two intelligent, basically self-centered, selfish human beings who share bed and board are going to have their "fights."

HOW DO YOU FIGHT FAIRLY?_____

You start by remembering that your mate is your best friend. Second, remember that unresolved conflict has a tendency to fester and grow instead of "just going away." Third, remind yourself that it's not who's right but what's right. Fourth, remember that regardless of who is at fault, the one who takes the first step to "make up" demonstrates more maturity. Also, understand that it might be a little awkward to bend over backward to please your mate, but there is very little chance you will fall on your face from that position.

Now for the "fight." Get two straight chairs and set them face to face about twenty-one inches apart. Next, you approach your mate and tell him or her that you want and need to have a friendly "fight" and that you've chosen a neutral battleground. Lead your mate to the designated chairs and take your seats facing each other.

If you are now mentally protesting that your mate would not go along with this, let me ask you if you've ever tried it. (I bet you haven't.) I'll also point out that if you follow this procedure early on in a disagreement (that's when you should) before it gets out of hand or before you build a "laundry list" of complaints, your mate not only will go along with you but will almost immediately see the humor and the practicality in the approach.

Now that you are seated face to face, you reach out and take hold of both your mate's hands (seated, face to face and holding hands, there's very little chance you will either hit each other or deal in bitter, vindictive name-calling or accusations). In a quiet voice you spell out the problems. Tell your

Word Fight at the O.K.* Corral

RULES:

1. Each person states (with emotion!): "YOU ARE MY BEST FRIEND!"

2. State together with emotion: "It is not *who* is right, but *what* is right!"

3. Think to yourself (you may close your eyes): "Unresolved conflict 'festers' and grows instead of just going away."

4. Determine to "bend over backward" in solving the "challenge" (so you will never fall on your face).

5. Sit in chairs twenty-one inches apart, hold hands, and make solid eye contact.

6. Regardless of who is at fault (don't place blame, fix the cause), someone begins. Remember that the one who takes the first step at reconciliation is demonstrating maturity.

7. Discuss the matter at hand. The angrier or more upset you become, the "slower and lower" you must speak.

8. Deal with issues, not personality. Make no personal attacks; deal with the facts. Not: "That was dumb . . ." or "You idiot . . ." Instead: "I felt disappointed . . ." or "This incident makes me feel . . ."

9. Arrive at a resolution or solution. If you can't, agree to return to the chairs and "fight again tomorrow."

10. Go to bed happy. The bed must be unmade before you get in, but you and your spouse should be "made up" before going to bed!

*We're both O.K., and this will make us better!

mate how you feel. Explain that you love him or her and you don't want anything to come between you.

When you are holding the flesh of the one you love, the chances of letting your "discussion" get out of hand are dramatically reduced. You will keep the "fight" on an issues basis and not on a personality basis. You'll be saying things like, "What you did really disappointed me," or "It really made me feel bad," instead of the personal attacks like, "That was a dumb thing you did!" or "I can't believe you said a thing like that!" What you want to do is keep the main issue as the main issue. Then you can discuss the facts carefully, calmly, and lovingly. That way your tempers and emotions are at least neutralized.

If no agreement or resolution can be reached that night, say, "Well, let's fight about this tomorrow," and since you're already holding hands and you're not going to sit in that chair all night, it will be quite natural for you to stand up and hug and kiss right where you are. This leads us to a most important point.

MAKE UP BEFORE YOU GO TO BED

One of the most disastrous events in a couple's married life is a fight that has not been resolved before going to bed. Now, that "fight" or conflict might have started at eight o'clock that morning or five o'clock that afternoon, but the rule is very clear: If that disagreement between husband and wife has left any discomfort, hurt, or bitterness between them, they absolutely must make up before they go to bed. First of all, it's the only way either will get a decent night's sleep. Second, if the cause of anger is allowed to stay in the mind and heart, then it settles into the subconscious mind, "festers," and makes making up all the more difficult.

If you have determined to resume the "fighting" the next day, you must "make up" for the fighting already covered. No sandbagging ("hold-over" complaints) allowed. Clear the air on all the issues presented.

Remember that early on in *Courtship* I discussed the fact that you made a commitment to each other, and that commitment is to seek reconciliation in the event there are serious disagreements. Most problems in marriage are nit-picking little incidentals that "don't really amount to a hill of beans." Oftentimes stubbornness and pride enter the picture, and the husband and/or wife just absolutely refuse to apologize and seek that forgiveness. Obviously, a stable marriage can survive one of those incidents or, for that matter, many of them. But every one takes its toll, and the day will come when the feeling for each other will diminish to the point that you have a marriage in name only, certainly not a relationship.

My good friend, the late Dick Gardner, often corrected a very popular statement when he would remind us that a lot of people used the phrase, "Life is too short for that." The reality is, life is too long for us to go through it harboring resentments and little grudges or petty incidents that create disharmony within the marriage. The rule is clear: If there is a disagreement that is unresolved, whether the disagreement was "major" or "minor," the issue needs to be resolved before you get into bed if you expect to get a good night's sleep.

FACE THE BATTLE—WIN THE WAR

By now it should be crystal clear that I'm talking about minor skirmishes or brushfires and not all-out war. However, most marital wars start out as small problems that simply grew and got out of control. If you and your mate are in serious difficulty, I encourage you to do more than I've discussed so far. A trained Christian counselor, psychologist, or psychiatrist can be a real marriage saver. I've seen some marriages not only saved but put back together in such a manner that they actually flourished. Oftentimes the husband and wife are so emotionally involved they are blind to the problem and have become so irrational they feel that the only alternative is divorce or the mate's 100 percent change because it is all the other's fault.

As you think about what happens in a disagreement with a spouse, you will begin to realize the importance of husbands and wives becoming best friends. You might fight with and vow to never forgive or "make up" with your mate, but if your mate is also your best friend, you will be willing, even anxious, to take the necessary steps, including counseling, to solve the problem.

COUNSELING *CAN* HELP

This next story illustrates what I'm talking about as far as counseling is concerned. The story is true; the advice is sound and simple. It worked and a marriage was saved. Your marriage is worth saving, and surely you will agree that counseling at least should be tried as a viable alternative. If it works, look what you've gained; if it doesn't work, you've lost nothing by trying.

Don Hawkins, who spent almost twenty years in the pastorate, tells a story of the time a couple from his church came to see him—en route as a last stop before seeing their respective lawyers about a divorce. It seems the husband had become involved in an affair. His wife became angry and decided to retaliate in kind. According to Don, the tension was electric. The husband sat on one side of the room hurling accusations. The wife sat on the other side, cold as ice, but occasionally blasting away with bitter fireball-type epithets at him.

Don suggested to this couple that they take one of the actions I'm recommending in *Courtship*, namely, to start over. Go back to that point in time where they were in love. To which the man replied, "But I don't love her anymore."

Don said to the man, "You do respect the Bible, don't you?"

"Yes," he replied.

"Well, Scripture says, 'Love Your Wife.'"

"Yes, but we're not living together as husband and wife. We have separate bedrooms."

"Oh, you're living in rooms next to each other?"

"That's right."

"Well, Scripture has a word for you, 'Love Your Neighbor.'"

The young man retorted, "I don't feel like she's a neighbor. We relate to each other more like enemies."

To which Don replied enthusiastically, "That's great. I have good news for you. Scripture covers that base as well. It says, 'Love Your Enemies.'"

Both husband and wife told Don, "But we just don't feel like loving each other, and we certainly wouldn't want to be hypocritical, would we?"

Don said, "Why don't we suspend the discussion of hypocrisy for a week? Let me encourage you to go back to treating each other like you loved each other."

To the husband he said, "You call her from work." To the wife he said, "You have a nice meal prepared." And to both he said, "Speak kind words to each other, even try to show some physical affection with an occasional hug or touch of the hands. Let's see what happens in a week's time."

The following week, the couple returned to Don's office. He was surprised to note that instead of taking seats on the opposite side of the office, both sat down on the same couch. Turning to the husband, Don asked, "What's the deal?"

To which the wife replied, "He's been nicer to me than he's been since we were married ten years ago."

Smiling, the husband said, "I guess you can love your enemy."

Now, I don't want to mislead you. As Don shared this with me, he was careful to point out that this couple's problems didn't just disappear overnight or vanish like a fog in the morning sun. There was a lot of hard work to do to resolve the conflicts, anger, bitterness, and hurt that had built up over years of marital neglect. Yet by turning to the kind of actions they practiced for each other in the very beginning, by starting the courtship process over—they became motivated to work on their marriage relationship.

STACK THE ODDS IN YOUR MARRIAGE'S FAVOR

There's a great line from an old Jimmy Stewart film called *Shenandoah*. Stewart, playing the part of a crusty family patriarch from the South, has several sons and one very special daughter. A young Confederate officer is actively seeking the young lady's hand in marriage. Finally, getting a requested audience with Stewart, the young man comes right to the point, "Sir, I want to marry your daughter."

To which Stewart caustically replies, "Why should I let my daughter marry you?"

The young man's response is almost instant, "Because I love her."

To which Stewart, after pausing for emphasis, retorts, "Loving her, that's not what's important. You've gotta like her."

That's a lot of what's involved in being best friends—liking each other; sharing events, circumstances, and even little random thoughts; developing and cultivating that sense of closeness with each other. The end result, as Dr. Howard Hendricks puts it, is that *you're married not to someone you can live with, but to someone you really cannot live without.*

Three things that greatly increase the odds of a successful marriage: (1) Pray together aloud daily; (2) read your Bible together every day; and (3) attend church regularly together.

All the factors I've mentioned are important for making sure husband and wife will function together in harmony. Having properly designated roles with the husband as leader, resolving conflicts by fighting fairly, becoming each other's cheerleader or encourager, becoming each other's best friend—all these are important. But there's a final and essential principle underscored by Dr. Richard Furman, author of *The Intimate Husband.* He says that if you do three things, the odds are two hundred to one that your marriage will make it. Number one, pray together aloud on a daily basis. Number two, read your Bible together every day. Number three, regularly attend church services together.

DON'T WASH YOUR DIRTY LINEN IN PUBLIC

When there are problems, and most marriages have a few major ones as well as a number of minor ones, one of the most foolish—and certainly one of the most tragic—causes of serious problems comes about because a husband and/or wife involve friends, relatives, neighbors and, for that matter, complete strangers or anybody within earshot. The sad thing about telling stories about your marriage difficulties, particularly if there are two or three interested, sympathetic listeners, is that you will have a tendency to embellish your comments and "stack" the evidence on your side.

Don't wash your dirty linen in public.

Chances are excellent that despite your pleas to them to not let anybody know, these individuals many times simply cannot resist the temptation to share this inside information. It gives them a feeling of importance to know they have been "trusted" with such intimate details of a serious disagreement between the "ideal couple." The tragedy is that in countless numbers of cases, the husband and wife solve their problems but face needless embarrassment and pressure because their friends, neighbors, coworkers, and family know all about their problems and have chosen sides.

When you have a serious disagreement and one or both parties consider that you need to back away and temporarily separate, you definitely need to—and should—talk about the situation to someone who is in a position to give you some sound advice on steps to take. You might speak to your parents or your priest or minister. You might see a Christian psychologist or simply an older, wiser, more gentle and understanding person.

I caution you that if your parents were opposed to the marriage in the beginning, they might have a little difficulty in being objective about the situation. I encourage you to use caution and discretion in choosing a person you want to share this information with. If your motive is to heal the relationship, hold the marriage together, and even improve the marriage, you definitely want to share only with someone who has experience or some insights that qualify the individual to give you advice and counsel.

The objective is to salvage and improve the marriage. With this in mind, you will give a much more balanced view of the difficulty and specifically what led to the problems. There are seldom circumstances where one person is 100 percent at fault and the other is completely innocent. The *only* time you talk about your problems is when you are sharing them with a person who is qualified to help and your objective is to solve the problem and not to build support for your case.

Obviously, the extent and nature of the disagreement will play a significant role as to whom you should seek for counseling and what action you should take. I'll have to confess that on this issue I carry a large amount of prejudice. If there is physical abuse, in the overwhelming majority of the cases (though certainly not in 100 percent) it is the husband who has abused the wife.

FACE THE PROBLEM

If the husband has abused the wife, I'm convinced that the *first* time this happens, regardless of whether or not he was "drunk and didn't know what he was doing" or "out of his mind on drugs," you should make your departure from that environment immediately. You should go to a shelter for battered women if there are no relatives close by so that you and your children, if there are any, can be safe until the offending mate cools off or sobers up. You should *immediately* have him in counseling before you even discuss going back to him. Historically speaking, the man who abuses his wife regrets it deeply, vows he will never do it again, can't imagine what got into him, loves you deeply, says you're the most important person on the face of the earth to him, states he absolutely could not live without you, declares he'll do anything you want him to do, give you anything you want to have, if you will only come back immediately. *Don't do it!*

Chances are excellent at that moment he means exactly what he says, but one of two things will be true. Either he is "sick" and really *can't* do anything about it, or he is "just downright mean and deceitful" and *won't* do anything about it. In either case, you need to protect yourself and, if there are children, protect those children. If no money is available to pay for counseling, the public health department or community services will provide counseling. Many Christian ministers have also been trained in that area. Again I say: Before you return to your abusive, violent mate, absolutely insist he have counseling. Don't go rushing back at the first call.

I know of one specific case, for example, where a lady lived with an alcoholic husband for thirty years. He made repeated promises that he was never going to hurt her again. He abused her and neglected the children. Though he was a good man when he was sober, he simply was drunk too often.

Finally, after thirty years, she had "had enough." She moved out and left him high and dry. All of his pleas wouldn't bring her back. A short time later, he made a commitment to Jesus Christ as his Lord and Savior and truly became a new man. He went back to his wife and pleaded with her to come back, but over a period of time she'd heard too many pleas and too many promises. She told him if he remained sober and faithful for a year, then she would move back with him. During the succeeding months he courted her just as avidly and enthusiastically as he had before they were married, but they didn't live as man and wife. After the year, when she could tell he genuinely had changed, she moved back again, and they had a magnificent marriage with much love and affection until the day of his death.

The story did have a happy ending, but isn't it tragic that the husband was abusive and that the wife didn't realize she could force him to take responsibility by taking a stand?

Confronting a problem in marriage doesn't always solve it, but until problems are confronted, few, if any, of them just go away.

FORGIVE *OR* FORGET

I emphasize that the reason the story had a happy ending was the fact that the wife totally and completely forgave her husband for all of those years of drunkenness, pain, and misery that he had brought upon both of them and the rest of the family. Had the forgiveness not been there, he might have stopped drinking, but there would have been no joy or excitement in that marriage. They simply would have signed a "non-aggression pact" and would have existed under the same roof; however, their feelings would not have been those of a loving couple.

This success story then has two key factors. First, the man repented of his sins and wrongdoings. He asked for forgiveness, and it was granted. Because she forgave, the marriage was restored, and they were able to enjoy those last few years together. They *both* won because of her forgiveness. Second, the message is clear—when the "fight" or difficulty is truly over, forgiveness on both parts is necessary if the marriage is to survive and be happy.

The *American Dictionary of the English Language*, the Noah Webster 1828 edition, says that *to forgive* is "to pardon; to overlook an offense and treat the offender as not guilty." There is a deep and very practical reason for forgiving your mate. When that fight is over or a wrong has been committed, in Matthew 6:14–15 in *The Everyday Bible* translation, we read, "Yes, if you forgive others for the things they do wrong, then your Father in heaven will also forgive you for the things you do wrong. But if you don't forgive the wrongs of others, then your Father in heaven will not forgive the wrong things you do."

Once you have forgiven your mate, you need to forgive yourself. Many times, over the years, your mate has perhaps blamed you for the problems, as was probably the case in the above example. When that happens, guilt feelings creep in. Just to make certain everything is open and you are completely freed, you need to forgive yourself and ask your mate to forgive you for the part you might have played in the difficulties. This completely clears the air *and* hearts so you can get back to the pleasures and benefits of courting your mate with all obstacles removed.

This is possible because forgiveness in its purest form means being released from the effects of the wrong we have done. Forgiveness extends love when punishment or hostility may be deserved. Forgiveness replaces rejection with acceptance and relinquishes the right to revenge. Above all, forgiveness chooses not to continue to bring up the failures of the past.

When moral failures have occurred, particularly if adultery or abuse is involved, true forgiveness is so difficult that counseling is often necessary to help untangle the feelings of guilt, rejection, blame, anger, and hurt. Since we are flesh and blood and not computers, when we've been emotionally hurt like abuse and adultery hurt us, forgiveness is a choice that is difficult to make. However, since the options make it clear as to which one is the wisest, I encourage you to think it through very carefully.

You might "feel" that he or she "deserves" punishment, not forgiveness. It's easy to understand those feelings, but the reality is that if there is no forgiveness, there will be little, if any, peace of mind or happiness. With forgiveness, chances are dramatically improved that the marriage can be saved. Then over a period of time, when the mate proves that he or she really has changed and truly is regretful, the marriage can again be beautiful and happy. It won't be easy, but since only 10 percent of the couples who divorce are genuinely happy ten years later, forgiveness and restoration of the marriage seem to be the better choice.

Many times we have been told to forgive and to forget, but the advice should be to forgive *or* forget about having any chances of having a restored and loving marriage. The reality is that forgetting, particularly so close to the time of being abused or learning of a moral failure, is not only difficult; it is impossible. However, over a period of time, though you never completely forget, your memory bank begins to refill with the positive, loving occasions, and you start to focus on the good instead of the hurt. Eventually, your hurt will grow so dim in your memory that only a specific incident will bring it back. Then the thought will be a brief one.

Carefully and prayerfully read the beautiful words of Robert Muller, former assistant secretary-general of the United Nations, who wrote them for International Forgiveness Week (which I believe begins every Sunday at 12:00 A.M. and extends to every Saturday at 12:00 P.M.):

DECIDE TO FORGIVE

Decide to forgive
For resentment is negative,
Resentment is poisonous,
Resentment diminishes and devours the self.
Be the first to forgive,
To smile and to take the first step,
And you will see happiness bloom
On the face of your human brother or sister.
Be always the first;
Do not wait for others to forgive.
For by forgiving
You become the master of fate,
The fashioner of life,
The doer of miracles.
To forgive is the highest,
Most beautiful form of love.

In return you will receive
Untold peace and happiness.
Here is the program for achieving a truly forgiving heart:

Sunday:	Forgive yourself.
Monday:	Forgive your family.
Tuesday:	Forgive your friends and associates.
Wednesday:	Forgive across economic lines within your own nation.
Thursday:	Forgive across cultural lines within your own nation.
Friday:	Forgive across political lines within your own nation.
Saturday:	Forgive other nations.

Only the brave know how to forgive. A coward never forgives. It is not in his nature.

11 | LOVE NEVER FAILS

Love is something we all yearn for, and to love and be loved is the most blissful state imaginable. But what is love? The best definition, I feel, is caring as much for the aims and welfare of another person as you do about your own aims and well-being. During my late husband's long illness, I realized that I would have gladly given up my own life if his would be saved, and I knew how deeply a woman could love. Too may people mistake the sweaty palms and dizzy exhilaration of a romantic encounter for love.

—Dr. Joyce Brothers

As a young sailor in the Naval Air program during World War II, I had been assigned to attend Millsaps College in Jackson, Mississippi, prior to going into flight training. One Friday evening, I went to the YWCA because young ladies from the area hosted weekly socials and there were refreshments. At that stage of my life I had a considerable interest in both young ladies and refreshments so I invested my nickel in the three-mile bus ride and I was on my way. The fact that this particular Friday night was the only time I ever went to the YWCA and the only time Jean Abernathy went to the YWCA leads us both to *know* that God's hand was involved in bringing us together.

A few minutes after 9:00 P.M., on September 15, 1944, I walked into the Jackson YWCA, and what should I see standing by the nickelodeon (a "jukebox" for you young "whipper-snappers," a pay-for-play C.D. unit for you *younger* folks) but a vision of loveliness—five feet two inches of femininity with long auburn hair down to her shoulders. At that instant I knew my search was over—at least for the evening.

I went over to her and with considerable originality

217

said, "Hi." She responded with the same originality, "Hi." I then asked her to dance. Though the thought of dancing frightened me, the thought of standing that close to someone that attractive enabled me to overcome my fear. She accepted, and I was thrilled! Within a few minutes, we were happily engaged in an argument of monumental proportions, discussing some matter of world-shattering importance. Happily, the twinkle in her eyes and the smile on her face indicated the disagreement was a very pleasant experience, and we were off to the races. Fortunately, she was spending the night with a close friend of hers, Dot Capps, who lived across the street from the Millsaps campus. When the festivities were over, we rode the bus home. I secured her phone number, and romance was definitely in bloom.

LOVE OR FASCINATION

To be candid, I was absolutely fascinated with Jean Abernathy from the moment I met her. Deep down I felt the relationship would extend beyond that first evening. I was enormously attracted to her, but to say I loved her or she loved me borders on the ridiculous. "Instant love" happens in the movies and on television, but much more rarely in real life. When love doesn't happen as quickly, easily, or painlessly as in movies or television, some people get discouraged, which in my opinion is a contributing factor to much of our marital discord today. That's not to say that instant love is impossible, but it is highly improbable. In the rare case of a two-week romance turning into a forty-year marriage, I'm convinced the people involved were infatuated with each other when they married and courted each other until they fell in love. Generally speaking, though, you don't fall in love at first sight; you might fall "in lust," but not in love.

At the end of a month, however, I honestly thought I loved Jean Abernathy; at the end of six months I *knew* I loved her; at the end of a year there was zero doubt about it—it was the relationship that would last forever! At any rate, that's what I believed.

The reality is, at that stage of my life, I did not have a clue as to what real love is all about. Psychiatrist Ross Campbell says it takes two years for a person's character to be fully revealed. The person you date under ideal circumstances a few times is oftentimes not the individual you would be willing or able to spend the rest of your life with. To fully understand another human being, you need to go through two full years of seasons—winter, spring, summer, and fall. You need to see your beloved under all kinds of social, business, and family situations in order to fully know that person's character. Only then can you really begin to appreciate and explore the depths of love.

A CLOSER LOOK

In two years, most of a person's character will have been revealed. You will have seen the person feeling good and not so good; you probably will have seen the person's tears and heard the laughter; you will have seen the person well-rested and, on occasion, very tired. You will have been together under ideal circumstances and circumstances not so ideal.

You will come to know whether the person is very generous or very tight. You will know whether the person loves children and pets or holds them at arm's length. You will know about faith and moral values. You will know how the person gets along with family and friends. You will know about health habits and educational interests and background. You will learn whether you're comfortable or uncomfortable with that person in the presence of others. You will clearly know whether or not you will be proud to introduce that person to all of your friends and family, or whether or not that person would be an embarrassment to you under certain circumstances. You will be able to determine whether or not this is the man or woman you really want to choose as the father or mother of your children. In short, although this is no guarantee of marital success, a two-year courtship does give you a significantly larger amount of information so the decision you make will not be based entirely on those "hoppin' hormones" that are unreliable, at best, and deceitfully dangerous, at worst.

Now, since the majority of you are already married, why spend this much time on the "pre-marriage courtship"? First, to enable you to pass the information along to the "needy," and second, to put the proper perspective on how love matures.

MATURE LOVE OR IMMATURE LOVE

From a personal point of view, I can tell you I thought I loved The Redhead at the end of five years, and I did, to the extent of my ability to love at that stage of my life. The same can be said of ten years, fifteen years, and twenty years. But the reality is that we had been married over twenty-five years before I fully came to know what love was all about. That happened after I committed my life to Jesus Christ on July 4, 1972. When I learned to love through Him, I experienced real love that continues to grow.

Dr. Joyce Brothers points out, "I have found that as love matures, it grows better, warmer, deeper." Eric Fromm contrasts mature love with infantile in the following fashion: "Infantile love follows the principle: I love because I am loved. Mature love follows the principle: I am loved because I love."

Mature love takes action and meets the other's needs, but it isn't trying to totally rescue someone else or meet every single need, as Dr. Beatriz Dujoven puts it:

> Mature love can flourish only between two people who feel whole and worthwhile as individuals. Love is not possible when one partner is expected to fill the other's inner voids. "If you really loved me, you wouldn't need other people" is another expression of the desire to achieve the fusion we experienced with our mothers as babies.

In other words, that's not mature love; it's immature.

WHAT IS THIS THING CALLED LOVE?

We use the word *love* to convey many different ideas. We speak of loving God, loving people, loving pets, loving food: "I love homemade ice cream," for example, or "I just love my new dress."

In his series of Bible studies for couples titled "Two Become One," J. Allan Petersen lists four words that give us a different perspective on kinds of love. The first of these is *stergo*, which he describes as a love that is inherent in one's own nature. This is the kind of love a parent has for offspring. It can be, and often is, sacrificial.

One story tells how a mother hen and all her chicks were walking in the barnyard when a storm blew up. The mother hen gathered all her chicks under her and sat on them as the rain began to fall. As the storm worsened, the hail was large and hit the mother hen with much force, but she remained there on top of her chicks. Finally, the hail came down so hard it beat the mother hen to death. Yet, after the storm, all the chicks crawled out from under the hen unharmed. She had sacrificed her life for them.

A second kind of love described by Petersen is *eros*. Although as it is used in our modern culture, eros usually carries a negative connotation; it can be either good or bad. Its basis is primarily in the physical, triggered by emotion. Eros is the heart of sexual desire and romantic feelings. As we have already seen, the Bible has a lot of positive things to say about this kind of love.

When we are visually attracted to another, this is the beginning of eros. Basically this comes from external stimulation. When I first saw The Redhead at the YWCA, I was attracted by her appearance. The better I got to know her, the more my feelings moved to the next kind of love.

The third kind of love described by Petersen is *phileo*. This kind of love involves a mutual attraction based on two individuals sharing things in common with each other—a fondness or a liking based on a similarity of outlook in life.

The Redhead and I found much "common ground" over the years, and as I have already mentioned, in 1972 we got on the best common ground of all—a personal relationship with Jesus Christ, which led us into the next kind of love.

The fourth, and easily the most basic and beautiful kind of love, is *agape*. Petersen describes this as "a love called out of one's heart by an awakened sense of value in the object loved that causes one to prize it." This love does not seek anything in return, not even acceptance of itself, but is first concerned for the other. It is the ultimate love, and it brings out the best in all of us.

This love letter nearly two thousand years ago from a Jewish scholar to his relatives in Corinth describes agape love. As a matter of fact, many people believe it is the most beautiful love letter ever written. He writes,

> If I speak in the tongues of men and of angels, but have not love, I am only a resounding gong or a clanging cymbal. If I

have the gift of prophecy and can fathom all mysteries and all knowledge, and if I have a faith that can move mountains, but have not love, I am nothing. If I give all I possess to the poor and surrender my body to the flames, but have not love, I gain nothing (1 Cor. 13:1–3 NIV).

And now listen as he describes what love really is all about:

Love is patient, love is kind. It does not envy, it does not boast, it is not proud. It is not rude, it is not self-seeking, it is not easily angered, it keeps no record of wrongs. Love does not delight in evil but rejoices with the truth. It always protects, always trusts, always hopes, always perseveres. Love never fails (1 Cor. 13:4–8 NIV).

And, of course, he's right.

At the end of each day, husbands and wives, we should ask ourselves these questions, "Was I patient with my mate today? Was I kind to my mate today? Was I envious of my mate today? Did I boast about what I had done, without regard to what my mate had done today?" Go right down the list, and I believe if each one of us will ask these questions, it will bring us into a more loving relationship with our mate.

THE TRUE LOVE DAILY CHECKLIST

1. Did I speak words of love to my mate today?
2. Did I act with love toward my mate today?
3. Was I patient with my mate today?
4. Was I kind to my mate today?
5. Was I jealous or envious of my mate today?
6. Was I boastful or proud of my mate today?
7. Was I selfish with or rude to my mate today?
8. Did I demand my own way with my mate today?
9. Was I irritable or "touchy" with my mate today?

10. Did I hold on to grudges with my mate today?
11. Was I glad when truth triumphed with my mate today?
12. Was I loyal to others with my mate today?
13. Did I believe in and expect the best from my mate today?
14. Did I use my strengths for my mate today?
15. Did I keep the faith with my mate today?
16. Did I find hope with my mate today?
17. Did I love my mate today?
18. Do I understand that the greatest strength is love?

A couple of important reminders: Love is not the basis for marriage; marriage is the basis for love. Being loved is the second-best thing in the world; loving someone is the best.

BETTER THAN EVER

Today, after 26 years of marriage I am more sensitive to the thrill of her presence than I have ever been. When I come on her unexpectedly in a crowd, it is like a glad little song rising up somewhere inside me. When I catch her eye in public, it is as though she were hanging out a sign with the exact word of inspiration I need right then. When I drive home in the evening, I must consciously guard the foot pedal, lest I step on the gas a little too fast as I approach the house where she waits for me. I still count it the biggest thrill when she comes hurrying from wherever she is to greet me, and, as I look down the road ahead, I see an elderly man and woman going into the sunset hand in hand. I know in my heart that the end will be better than the beginning.

Charlie Shedd wrote those words over a quarter of a century ago, and they proved to be prophetic. The marriage continued to grow, and the love continued to increase. After over fifty years of marriage, his beloved died in his arms, thus ending a beautiful romance of over a half-century. How wonderful to know the romance will be resumed when Charlie joins his wife in eternity!

LOVE COULD—OFTEN DOES—AND DEFINITELY SHOULD—GROW

In some ways, of course, many people would say that Charlie and Martha Shedd's story is most unusual, but I, for one, can certainly relate. I vividly remember about five years ago when I was speaking in Little Rock, Arkansas, and fully expected to spend the night there. However, the seminar sponsor told me we would be finishing early and I could catch an earlier flight home. I was elated and decided to surprise The Redhead by showing up without calling. The connection was close, and when I arrived, there were no seats on the plane. It wasn't until the last minute that as a standby passenger, I got aboard the flight. Feeling the excitement of a schoolboy, I anticipated the reaction of my "bride" when her "happy husband" showed up at home. The plane landed at the airport; I made my way to my automobile and took off for home.

Normally, I'm a reasonably safe, responsible driver so I was somewhat chagrined on the stretch from the airport into the outskirts of Dallas when I glanced down and noticed the speedometer was approaching eighty miles an hour. The first thing I did was take my foot off the gas pedal; the second thing I did was literally laugh out loud. It hit me in a beautiful fashion that I really did have a crush on The Redhead. I felt like that schoolboy on his first date. Yes, the incident does have a happy ending. The Redhead was not only surprised but delighted to welcome me home.

I believe that kind of relationship with your mate is highly possible. It won't be easy. It will require effort, but I can assure you that you won't be "sacrificing" anything. You'll be making a series of small investments that will pay lifetime dividends.

LEARNING TO LOVE

I believe love is learned, but learning to love is different from learning to ride a bicycle or work mathematical problems. However, love is learned, and some folks fail in love because they never learn how to love. Here are some practical suggestions to help you learn. First, don't "save" enjoyable times for special occasions; work on sharing them daily. Let your loved one know that you enjoy the time you share simply because you're spending it together.

Look for, and you'll find, activities you both enjoy and will enjoy even more together. Others that you don't enjoy doing by yourself can be a delight when you do them together (washing and drying dishes, or even cleaning out closets, for example). Take a walk, play tennis, plant a garden, or even wash your car—together. The important thing is that you share work and play time together on a regular basis.

Of considerably more importance is the fact that you need to learn as much as you can about the object of your love. Real love reaches its zenith when two people are perfectly content just being together. That's why a reasonably long courtship before marriage is always advisable—and courtship *after* marriage is essential.

What happens when we love? What are the effects and the results? John Drexler says, "When we love each other, we make each other lovely. When we honor each other, we make each other honorable. When we respect each other, we make each other respectable."

According to Neil Strait, "The balm of love is such a powerful, helpful ingredient that when it is applied, life is strengthened and nurtured to a new level of living." Ann Landers describes love as "an upper. It makes you look up. It makes you think up. It makes you a better person than you were before."

William Arthur Ward observes that "love gives life its purpose, meaning and direction. Love provides life with joy, flavor, laughter, excitement and beauty. Love causes us to give, to sacrifice, to serve and to sing. And love ultimately makes a marriage work."

Ken Druck, Ph.D., writing in *Family Circle*, states, "In the fifteen years I have been counseling couples, I have found that the happiest—and strongest—marriages are those in which the spouses are lovers, friends, partners in maintaining a lifestyle." In other words, a balanced marriage, undergirded by love, is one in which both parties "learned to stop taking each other—and their separate identities—for granted." Those marriages really click.

REAL—NOT COUNTERFEIT—LOVE _____

A number of years ago, The Redhead went to the bank to make a deposit following one of our public seminars. The teller was counting the money, and they do count it quickly. The young lady behind the counter had a stack of twenty-dollar bills, and she was counting a mile a minute when suddenly she stopped, reached down, picked up one of the twenty-dollar bills, and said, "Mrs. Ziglar, this is a counterfeit twenty-dollar bill." She had recognized that it was counterfeit immediately because in most banks they will not permit tellers to even touch anything but the real thing. That way, when they do encounter a counterfeit bill, they can instantly recognize the difference in the feel.

Unfortunately in our society today, it is not quite as easy to separate real love from the counterfeit variety. As I have already mentioned, our young people see the television or movie version of love that is presented as "the real thing." In reality those shows depict a relationship between a boy and a girl who meet, establish a "meaningful" relationship (they go to dinner first), and then go to bed. As you might suspect, they often declare their "love," and since they are skillful actors, their actions often come across to a naive youngster as being "the real thing." In reality what they've experienced is infatuation, which Ann Landers identifies as "instant desire. It is one set of glands calling to another. Love (on the other hand) is friendship that has caught fire; it takes root and grows—one day at a time."

Love as described by Neil Strait is "the greatest exercise the heart can engage in. It is the one exercise that makes all of life a little better."

That must have been Charlie Shedd's thought when he wrote, concerning his relationship with his wife, "Every day we will give each other some simple compliment. Nothing stupendous here, but then again, multiply it by many years and it is colossal!"

MORE BEAUTIFUL THAN EVER

For a number of years, as I have traveled the country making presentations to audiences of all kinds and sizes, I've made the observation that my wife is more beautiful today than she was on our wedding day. To tell you the truth, that statement bothered me, and there's a distinct possibility it bothered some of the people in the audience. It did not bother me because I felt I was stretching the truth or exaggerating, but the improbability bothered me. Like most men my age, I like to think I'm practical and realistic, and to state that a "mature" grandmother in her sixties is more beautiful than an eighteen-year-old bride just simply defies all rhyme or reason. Yet, in my mind, the statement was definitely true.

The mystery was completely cleared up in 1986 when I was part of a group that took a trip to Israel. I'll confess that the emotion of the moment might have played a part; perhaps it was because I had read the "Sermon on the Mount" on the exact spot where Christ is said to have delivered that sermon. Maybe it was because I had walked on the shore and sailed on the Sea of Galilee, where so much of His ministry had taken place. Maybe it was because I had peered into the tomb, where He is believed to have been entombed, and looked at Golgotha, where His crucifixion took place.

All of these things are, of course, possible, but on Sunday morning, as we sat there in Jerusalem in a church service in our hotel, Pastor Ben Glosson, a Baptist preacher from Hazlehurst, Georgia, was preaching a magnificent sermon on our Lord. Since Ben also has a beautiful singing voice, he injected "How Great Thou Art" into the sermon. As I sat there, listening to that beautiful message in song, the awesomeness of what God had done for me was overpowering. With tears running down my cheeks, I was almost overcome with love and gratitude.

At that moment, it seemed the Lord spoke directly to me. That truly is a rare event for me, though I have felt on about seven or eight different occasions in the past years since my conversion that He has spoken to me in this way. Normally God speaks to me daily through His Bible, but that Sunday morning, as I sat there, He clearly impressed upon my mind why my wife is more beautiful in my eyes today than she was on our wedding day. He explained, as only a loving Father can, that He was now permitting me to see her through His eyes and, of course, our Lord sees us as perfect. What a magnificent experience that was! It clarified the mystery completely for me. Love, real love, truly is a beautiful experience. It is worth working for, waiting for, and praying for.

LOVE IS A BAKED SWEET POTATO

> You get married not to be happy but to make
> each other happy.
>
> —Roy L. Smith

When you and I got together over two hundred pages ago, we were both filled with certain expectations. I fully expected to share some insights with you that would not only make your marriage more fun and rewarding but do the same thing for your life.

Your expectations probably ranged from hoping to pick up a few neat ideas to expecting some miraculous cure for a desperately sick marriage. Regardless of what you expected, it is obvious that you found something encouraging or you would not have stayed with the book or be reading these words. The fact that you are still with me indicates that you are persistent, and that's a necessary quality for a successful, long-term marriage.

As we head into the closing pages of this book, I feel comfortably confident that the ideas and suggestions offered are sound and workable. I say this because many couples, over the years, have been most gracious in their comments concerning the benefit they received from attending my seminar or listening to my tapes on *Courtship After Marriage—Romance Can Last A Lifetime.*

Even as my editor was encouraging me to meet his deadline, I came across these words from Robert Fulghum in his book, *All I Really Need to Know I Learned in Kindergarten:*

> Share everything, play fair, don't hit people, put things back where you found them, clean up your own mess, don't take

things that aren't yours, say you're sorry when you hurt somebody, wash your hands before you eat, flush, cookies and cold milk are good for you—when you go out into the world, watch for traffic, hold hands and stick together.

That "sandbox" wisdom contains a wealth of information that will make any marriage a better one. If you will paste those words on your refrigerator and your bathroom mirror for regular reference, they will be helpful.

THREE SUGGESTIONS

The *Dallas Morning News*, on Sunday, November 26, 1989, carried an ultimate success story of courtship after marriage. The story detailed a fifty-year love affair between Doris Swann and Harold Y. Smith who eloped on November 24, 1939. Few who knew the young couple thought the marriage would last through the winter, let alone fifty years. The two had begun seeing each other at a small Bible college in Fort Worth, and Doris felt almost immediately that Harold was the "special someone" who would become the life companion she had dreamed of since childhood.

While helping a buddy pick out an engagement ring for his fiancee and with a few encouraging words from the jeweler, Harold bought a ring for Doris. Soon the young couple was engaged, and on that cold November Friday back in 1939, they eloped and were married by a justice of the peace in Cleburne, Texas. The event created quite a stir, and school officials predicted the marriage would soon collapse. However, the couple settled in Mt. Pleasant, Texas, in a home Harold constructed himself, and raised three children. Today Harold and Doris boast about their eleven grandchildren.

Their secret of success? As Doris told the *Dallas Morning News*, "It's been like walking down a yellow brick road with my sweetheart those fifty years." She added, "Happy marriages do not just happen; it takes work to make a successful marriage."

Three rules to make marriage last:
1. Love and serve God.
2. Remember choices, not circumstances, determine the flavor of our lives.
3. Live each day so that you'll never be afraid of tomorrow or ashamed of yesterday.

Doris and Harold believe their marriage has worked because they followed three rules over the years. Number one: Love and serve God. Number two: Remember choices, not circumstances, determine the flavor of our lives. Number three: Live each day so that you will never be afraid of tomorrow or ashamed of yesterday. I like that advice, and I love the fact that Doris and Harold Smith are now looking forward to reaching their seventy-fifth wedding anniversary—that's the result of courtship after marriage.

Harold and Doris Smith enjoy some special benefits that accompany a long-term marriage. The Redhead and I share their joy as it relates to grandchildren. And to be candid, if I had known those grandchildren were going to be so much fun, I certainly would have been nicer to their parents.

GRANDY'S SUNSHINE _____

One evening our granddaughter, Sunshine (her name is Amanda, but her bright and beautiful smile and shining intelligence make her "Sunshine" to those who know her), spent the night with The Redhead and me and was planning to spend a couple of days with us. I had been on a schedule no sane person would attempt, so I was pretty wrung out.

We slept the next morning until we woke up (come to think about it, that's what we always do!). We did sleep later than usual, and The Redhead suggested that I should "coast" for the day and we'd take Sunshine to the zoo. It didn't take much persuasion, so we dressed casually and headed for Le Peep, a Dallas restaurant famous for magnificent breakfasts. Sunshine ordered enough for any three normal adults, and together the two of us made substantial inroads into her meal. Then we headed for the zoo. We brought along our camera, and Sunshine was the official photographer for the day. She took all the pictures, except the ones she was in. She has made a scrapbook out of those pictures, and I'm confident that when she's a grandmother she will show her grandchildren those pictures.

About four delightful hours were involved at the zoo, and then we headed home. As we approached downtown Dallas, Sunshine saw Reunion Tower, a fifty-story skyscraper with a revolving restaurant on top, and excitedly asked, "Grandy, can we go up there and eat?" Since prices are in keeping with the height of the tower and it was far too early for dinner, we passed on the eating part, but we did agree to take her to the top of the tower and look the city over. The elevator ride was spectacular, and the view was magnificent. The wind is always blowing at that height, and the feeling was absolutely phenomenal. We spent a delightful thirty minutes looking at an awesome view of our city, and then we headed home. As we approached the house, Sunshine excitedly spoke up and said, "Grandy, let's go hit some golf balls!" Since Sunshine is such a smooth talker, we headed for the club that is close to the house. We had fun for about thirty minutes hitting those golf balls, and then we returned home.

Grandmothers

A grandmother is a little girl who's had more time to grow up than anybody! One of her greatest assets is age—she's lived through three to six generations, and experience is a wise teacher. A small boy knows he can bring his troubles to his grandmother and she'll understand. She never expects a boy to be perfect the way a mother sometimes does. A little girl knows no one can tell better stories, make prettier doll clothes, or serve sweeter cookies. Troubles fade in her arms. The world isn't nearly as frightening a place when she's there. And she can always be counted on to take the underdog's part. Lucky, indeed, is the child who can carry a good grandmother image into the long hard years ahead.

—Ester Winship Snyder

After a brief period of rest and relaxation, we went out to dinner, had a marvelous time, and finally called it quits that night at about eleven o'clock.

I've thought about that day any number of times and have remembered our time with our "Sunshine" girl with much pleasure and excitement. The sobering thought is this: Had The Redhead and I, for whatever reason, broken our relationship earlier in our lives, that particular day would never have happened.

That's not to say that divorced people never see their children, but it is definitely true that many, many of the normal joys of family are denied: Vacation times are different; Christmas, Thanksgiving, New Year's, birthdays, anniversaries, Valentine's Day, the Fourth of July, Labor Day, graduations, school parties, ball games, social occasions, visits with friends, spontaneous trips to ball games, museums, or zoos, and ten thousand other things no longer are quite the same—or even possible. They simply do not fit into the new scheme of things. New husbands, wives, children, in-laws, and grandparents present an endless series of new and different challenges.

THE JOY NEVER CEASES

On yet another summer day, The Redhead was in Shreveport to be with her sister following surgery, and I was working in my office at home, feeling a little lonely. (Actually I was having a pity party. And as you may know, the only problem with a pity party is that no one shows up but you, and there are no refreshments.) I called my granddaughter, "Keeper" (when a fisherman pulls in a good one, he's got a "keeper," and when we first saw Katherine Jean Alexandra Witmeyer, we knew she was a "keeper"), and asked her if she wanted to spend the night with me. With considerable excitement and enthusiasm, she accepted the invitation. I was delighted because circumstances are such that I seldom have the opportunity to spend an entire evening with one of my grandchildren.

In addition, as children get older and more independent they have less time for their parents and grandparents—unless we develop a relationship and plant the seeds of spending time when they are younger. So I rushed over and picked her up. We did not come straight home but stopped to enjoy a scoop of ice cream. We got home and took a little walk. Since Keeper is a talker and I've been known to say a few things myself, we had a delightful visit. We sat around and chatted and talked and played for a while. Then at about ten o'clock, she gave solid evidence of being ready for bed, so I tucked her in. I still had some work to do, so I worked for a couple of hours.

As I prepared for bed, I paused for a moment to look at that beautiful little girl, curled up, sound asleep, in complete contentment and trust. She was at peace with herself and felt perfectly secure. As I looked at her and leaned down to kiss her cheek and stroke her hair, I could not help but think that had The Redhead and I separated at any stage of our lives, this little vignette would never have happened, and both our lives would have been poorer because of it.

As you either begin or continue to apply the principles shared in this book, you increase your chances of enjoying the "extended family."

LOVE IS A BAKED SWEET POTATO

There's an excellent chance you will be stunned—or at least surprised—that I have chosen to end this book, and specifically this chapter, with this final little analogy. However, I believe by the time we're through, you will agree that it was a good choice.

You might, at this point, be thinking to yourself, "But

how on earth could love be a baked sweet potato?" so let me tell you about the baked sweet potato. We start with a potato about the size of a man's fist. If it's larger than that, the sweet potato will probably be grainy, and if it's too small, it will be stringy. We bake this potato in a moderately hot oven because if it's too hot the skin will dry out and won't be good to eat. That would be a real loss because, actually, the skin is the best part of the potato.

Proper Preparation Produces Phantastic Potato

After baking the potato until it is nice and soft, remove it from the oven, slit it down the middle, and literally saturate it with gobs of polyunsaturated margarine (I sure hate to make that concession to cholesterol and eliminate that good ol' country butter!). Make absolutely certain that every nook and cranny of that potato is bathed in the margarine. To add anything else amounts to sacrilege and you will ruin one of God's most magnificent foods, so please don't add *anything* else to that potato.

The real connoisseurs of baked sweet potatoes would never dream of eating them along with a meal. The baked sweet potato is to be enjoyed either as a separate meal or as a dessert. Before you take the first bite, you rinse your mouth with good, cold water so that those taste buds are alive and poppin', which will enable you to achieve maximum enjoyment. You close your eyes for that first small bite of potato, and I can tell you, friend, if you've never experienced the ecstasy of that moment, you're in for a *real* treat—it's absolutely magnificent!

Would You Believe?

In my wildest imagination I cannot conceive of anyone not getting slightly emotional at the prospect of such a grand repast. However, incredibly enough, of all the people on earth, I happened to marry a lady who does not share my love, zest, zeal, passion, and enthusiasm for the baked sweet potato. That's not to say she dislikes them—it's just that she can either take them or leave them and, in most cases, she will leave them. I cannot imagine *that* happening to anybody, but most of all to me.

On the other hand, The Redhead's indifference to the baked sweet potato has a very positive benefit. When I walk in the front door of our home and I am hit right in the nose with the tantalizing, delicious, and splendidly beautiful aroma of the baked sweet potato, it really gets me excited! I know that fragrance has somehow slipped out of the oven and drifted to the floor of the kitchen where it made its way to the hallway. From there it turned left and, taking a short-cut through our living room, headed for the front door where it rose to greet me.

When that happens, I know The Redhead has been to the grocery store and has been thinking about me. And I know that when she picked up that potato, she was thinking about me. I know when she brought it home, she brought it home for me. I know that when she washed the potato, she did it just for me. As she tenderly placed that potato on the baking rack, she put it there just for me. I know that even as she turned the oven on, she again was thinking about me. The reason is obvious. As I stated earlier, she does not really relate to the baked sweet potato in the same way I do. She prepared that potato because of her love for me.

Yes, I'm convinced that love—real love—is a baked sweet potato. Now at this point you might well be thinking to yourself, "But, Zig! A baked sweet potato is such a little thing!" Now, obviously, I'd have to agree with that. But isn't that what love—real love—is all about? Love is truly a long series of little things that you do for your mate for no reason at all except the best reason of them all—you love and want to please your mate. When you do those "little things," like bak-

ing a sweet potato, you are unselfishly saying *I LOVE YOU!*
Our oft-quoted philosophy, "You can have everything in life
you want if you will just help enough other people get what
they want," is truer in the bonds of holy matrimony than any
other area of life.

Yes, love *is* a baked sweet potato, which, in a nutshell, is
simply one of the hundreds of little things loving mates seek
out to do for each other on a regular, daily basis. I'm convinced a stable, loving marriage will be built on a foundation
of little things that each of you do every day for the other. I
believe that if you will accept this idea, love and romance
will be alive as long as the marriage exists—and the marriage
will exist as long as you do.

APPENDIX A

Your Courtship After Marriage Survey

1. How did you happen to meet your mate?

   _____

2. What attracted you to him/her in the first place?

   _____

3. How long was the courtship process before the marriage took place?

   _____

4. Was your courtship procedure slowly developing?

   _____

5. Did you start out as just friends?

   _____

6. Did you grow up together as children?

   _____

7. Were you casual acquaintances at first?

   _____

8. How intimate was your relationship before marriage?

   (a) Physically _____

   (b) Mentally _____

   (c) Spiritually _____

9. Did both parents of the bride approve of the marriage?

   _____

10. Did both parents of the groom approve of the marriage?

    _____

11. Was the wedding a small, intimate family affair, involving fewer than twenty people, a small church wedding involving fewer than fifty, or was it a larger, more elaborate wedding (more than fifty)?

    _____

12. What was the major reason you married him/her?

    _____

13. What was, and is, the most exciting aspect of your marriage?

    _____

14. What was, or is, the most difficult aspect of your marriage?

    _____

15. Have there been any instances of violence or abuse, either physically or emotionally, or both, in your marriage?

_____

16. If yes, was it a onetime event or an ongoing occurrence?

_____

17. What is your spiritual faith?

_____

18. Are you and your mate of the same faith? If yes, what faith? If no, what are the differences in faith?

_____

19. Has your spiritual life been a definite "plus" in the marriage?

_____

20. Has your spiritual life created problems in the marriage?

_____

21. Do you attend church together regularly?

_____

22. Were there (are there) children in the marriage?

_____

If yes, how many? _____

23. What impact did children, if any, have on the marriage? Did they create problems or did they draw you closer together as a family?

   _____

24. Do either or both of you smoke, dip, or chew tobacco?

   _____

25. From an alcoholic beverage point of view, are you a "teetotaller," moderate drinker, or does alcohol present a problem for you?

   (a) Husband _____

   (b) Wife _____

26. Has alcohol caused problems in your marriage?

   _____

27. Have you used illegal drugs at any time in your life? If yes, are you still using them? Do they now or have they ever put a strain on your relationship?

   (a) Husband _____

   (b) Wife _____

28. Have you ever been separated? If so, what were the circumstances and how long was the separation?

_____

29. What kind of impact have in-laws had on your relationship? Have they been an asset or a liability?

_____

30. How often do you spend time with your in-laws?

_____

31. How much time have you spent apart during the marriage because of either of you traveling?

_____

32. Have both of you worked outside the home throughout the marriage, or has only one of you held an outside job?

_____

33. Have either of you worked part-time?

_____

34. In what ways are you and your mate similar?

_____

35. In what ways are you and your mate different?

_____

36. Did you go into marriage thinking you might change your mate in one way or another?

   _____

37. Who has the most control over how money is spent in your family?

   _____

38. Who pays the bills in your family?

   _____

39. Husband's age at marriage: _____

40. Wife's age at marriage: _____

41. Did either/both of you ever seriously consider divorce?

   _____

42. What one year of your marriage was the most difficult?

   _____

   Were there any extenuating circumstances that year?

   _____

43. What special challenges have you faced in your marriage, and how did/do you handle them? (Death of child, spouse's prolonged illness)

   _____

44. What kind of relationship did your parents have with each other, and what is your relationship with each of your parents?

(a) Husband _____

(b) Wife _____

*45. Who is the spiritual leader in your home?

_____

46. Concerning children, how do you rate yourself as a:

	FATHER	MOTHER
Strict	_____	_____
Moderate	_____	_____
Lenient	_____	_____

Do you believe in "corporal punishment"?

	FATHER	MOTHER
Yes	_____	_____
No	_____	_____

47. What have you done to keep romance alive in your relationship?

_____

*After you have finished reading this book, retake the last twenty-two questions (45–66) in the survey.

48. What are your favorite five things your mate does for you or with you that make you love and appreciate him/her more?

_____

49. Do you have any rules about meals, like requiring husband, wife, and children be together particularly for the evening meal?

_____

50. What are five things you do together as a couple that you most enjoy (in order, favorite activity first)?

_____

51. Do you remember birthdays, anniversaries, and other special occasions with cards, gifts, dinner out, or any other type of special recognition of the event? If yes, how?

_____

52. Do you give surprises on non-special occasions, for no reason other than the fact that you love one another?

_____

53. On a scale of 1 to 10, rate your mate on the following characteristics:

(a) Kind _____ (d) Considerate _____

(b) Thoughtful _____ (e) Gentle _____

(c) Helpful _____ (f) Romantic _____

(g)	Enthusiastic	____	(o) Spiritually strong	____
(h)	Positive	____	(p) Appreciative	____
(i)	Encouraging	____	(q) Good communicator	____
(j)	Sense of Humor	____	(r) Unselfish	____
(k)	Pleasant	____	(s) Interesting	____
(l)	Understanding	____	(t) Good provider/ homemaker	____
(m)	Spirit of cooperation	____	(u) Empathetic	____
(n)	Tolerant	____	(v) Good listener	____

54. **On a scale of 1 to 10, rate yourself on the same characteristics:**

(a)	Kind	____	(j) Sense of Humor	____
(b)	Thoughtful	____	(k) Pleasant	____
(c)	Helpful	____	(l) Understanding	____
(d)	Considerate	____	(m) Spirit of cooperation	____
(e)	Gentle	____	(n) Tolerant	____
(f)	Romantic	____	(o) Spiritually strong	____
(g)	Enthusiastic	____	(p) Appreciative	____
(h)	Positive	____	(q) Good communicator	____
(i)	Encouraging	____	(r) Unselfish	____

(s) Interesting   ____   (u) Empathetic   ____

(t) Good provider/   (v) Good listener   ____
     homemaker   ____

55. Do you regularly hold hands?

_____

56. Do you regularly hug each other throughout the day?

_____

57. Do you frequently tell your mate you love him/her?

_____

58. What is the number one thing you would change about
     your mate?

_____

59. Does money present a problem in your relationship?

_____

60. Is your marriage a partnership or does one usually give
     in to the other?

_____

61. Do you have the freedom in your marriage to share
     anger toward each other?

_____

62. Do you tell your mate how you feel about things he/she does that occasionally irritate you?

_____

63. Do you strive to accept your mate, just the way he/she is right now?

_____

64. Do you feel like your mate strives to accept you just the way you are right now, or does your mate use lots of "you should" or "you shouldn't" sentences in his/her communications with you?

_____

65. Do you consider your marriage a lifelong commitment? Does your mate?

_____

66. What advice or suggestions would you give young couples today as they embark on the sea of matrimony?

_____

APPENDIX B
Bibliography

I should warn you that I am a "traditionalist *and* a romanticist." I honestly believe that I am both because of the practicality involved. I will also confess to having a seriously sentimental side. However, in writing this book, I have been very careful in my research. I check *everything* psychologically, theologically, and physiologically before committing the facts to paper.*

Family Book Section

Blue, Ron and Judy. *Money Matters for Parents and Their Kids*. Nashville: Oliver-Nelson, 1988.

Chapin, Alice. *Building Your Child's Faith*. Nashville: Thomas Nelson, 1990.

Ketterman, Grace. *Depression Hits Every Family*. Nashville: Oliver-Nelson, 1988.

Mowday, Lois. *Daughters Without Dads*. Nashville: Oliver-Nelson, 1990.

Scott, Buddy. *Relief for Hurting Parents*. Nashville: Oliver-Nelson, 1989.

Stanley, Charles. *How to Keep Your Kids on Your Team*. Nashville: Oliver-Nelson, 1986.

Strack, Jay. *Dad, Do You Love Mom?* Nashville: Thomas Nelson, 1989.

Swindoll, Charles R. *You and Your Child, Expanded Edition*. Nashville: Thomas Nelson, 1990.

---

*This Bibliography contains the majority of the body of research I used in writing this book, plus some information recommended by friends and associates. I have not personally read each book, but trust those who have.

In addition, I would like to recommend reading any book written by these three authors: James Dobson, Archibald D. Hart, and Gary Smalley.

Management and Motivation

Blanchard, Kenneth, and Spencer Johnson. *The One Minute Manager*. New York: William Morrow and Company, Inc., 1982.

—— and Robert Lorber. *Putting the One Minute Manager to Work*. New York: William Morrow and Company, Inc., 1984.

Brown, W. Steven. *13 Fatal Errors Managers Make*. Old Tappan, N.J.: Fleming H. Revell Company, 1985.

Buck, Lee. *Tapping Your Secret Source of Power*. Old Tappan, N.J.: Fleming H. Revell Company, 1985.

Carnegie, Dale, and Associates. *Managing Through People*. New York: Simon & Schuster, Inc., 1978.

DeBruyn, Robert I. *Causing Others to Want Your Leadership*. Manhattan, Kan.: DeBruyn & Associates, 1976.

Gschwandtner, Gerhard. *Superachievers*. Englewood Cliffs, N.J.: Prentice-Hall, Inc., 1984.

Inspiration and Self-Help

Carnegie, Dale. *How to Stop Worrying and Start Living*. New York: Simon & Schuster, Inc., 1975.

——. *How to Win Friends and Influence People*. New York: Pocket Books, 1982.

Conwell, Russell. *Acres of Diamonds*. Old Tappan, N.J.: Fleming H. Revell Company, 1975.

Cooper, Kenneth, M.C. *The Aerobics Program for Total Well-Being*. New York: M. Evans, 1982.

Dobson, James. *What Wives Wish Their Husbands Knew*

About Women. Wheaton, Ill.: Tyndale House Publishers, 1975.

Maltz, Maxwell. *Psycho-Cybernetics*. New York: Pocket Books, 1970.

Mandino, Og. *The Greatest Miracle in the World*. New York: Bantam Books, 1977.

Marshall, Peter, and David Manuel. *The Light and the Glory*. Old Tappan, N.J.: Fleming H. Revell Company, 1977.

Peale, Norman Vincent. *The Power of Positive Thinking*. New York: Fawcett, 1978.

Schuller, Robert H. *Tough Times Never Last, but Tough People Do*. Nashville: Thomas Nelson Publishers, 1983.

Schwartz, David J. *The Magic of Thinking Big*. St. Louis: Cornerstone, 1962.

Smith, Fred. *You and Your Network*. Waco, Tex.: Word Books, 1984.

Other Books by Zig Ziglar

Confessions of a Happy Christian. Gretna, La.: Pelican, 1978.

Dear Family. Gretna, La.: Pelican, 1984.

Raising Positive Kids in a Negative World. Nashville: Thomas Nelson Publishers, Oliver-Nelson, 1985.

See You at the Top. Gretna, La.: Pelican, 1974.

Steps to the Top. Gretna, La.: Pelican, 1985.

Top Performance. Old Tappan, N.J.: Fleming H. Revell Company, 1986.

Zig Ziglar's Secrets of Closing the Sale. Old Tappan, N.J.: Fleming H. Revell Company, 1984.

For Your Continuing Education

Bits & Pieces. Published monthly by Economics Press, Inc., 12 Daniel Road, Fairfield, N.J. 07006.

Guideposts. Published monthly by Norman Vincent Peale and Ruth Stafford Peale, Carmel, N.Y. 10512.

Personal Selling Power. Published monthly by Gerhard Gschwandtner & Associates, P.O. Box 5467, Fredericksburg, Vir. 22403.

Reader's Digest. Published monthly by the Reader's Digest Association, Inc., Pleasantville, N.Y. 10570.